A Foreign Sound

33 1/3 Global

33 1/3 Global, a series related to but independent from **33 1/3**, takes the format of the original series of short, music-based books and brings the focus to music throughout the world. With initial volumes focussing on Japanese and Brazilian music, the series will also include volumes on the popular music of Australia/Oceania, Europe, Africa, the Middle East, and more.

33 1/3 Japan

Series Editor: Noriko Manabe

Spanning a range of artists and genres—from the 1960s rock of Happy End to technopop band Yellow Magic Orchestra, the Shibuya-kei of Cornelius, classic anime series *Cowboy Bebop*, J-Pop/EDM hybrid Perfume, and vocaloid star Hatsune Miku—**33 1/3 Japan** is a series devoted to in-depth examination of Japanese albums of the twentieth and twenty-first centuries.

Forthcoming titles:

Yoko Kanno's *Cowboy Bebop Soundtrack* by Rose Bridges

Perfume's *Game* by Patrick St. Michel

33 1/3 Brazil

Series Editor: Jason Stanyek

Covering the genres of samba, tropicália, rock, hip hop, forró, bossa nova, heavy metal, and funk, among others, **33 1/3 Brazil** is a series devoted to in-depth examination of the most important Brazilian albums of the twentieth and twenty-first centuries.

Forthcoming titles:

Tim Maia's *Tim Maia Racional Vols. 1 & 2* by Allen Thayer

João Gilberto and Stan Getz's *Getz/Gilberto* by Brian McCann

A Foreign Sound

Barbara Browning

33⅓ BRAZIL

Bloomsbury Academic
An imprint of Bloomsbury Publishing Inc.

B L O O M S B U R Y

NEW YORK · LONDON · OXFORD · NEW DELHI · SYDNEY

Bloomsbury Academic

An imprint of Bloomsbury Publishing Inc

50 Bedford Square	1385 Broadway
London	New York
WC1B 3DP	NY 10018
UK	USA

www.bloomsbury.com

BLOOMSBURY and the Diana logo are trademarks of Bloomsbury Publishing Plc

First published 2017

Library of Congress Cataloging-in-Publication Data
Names: Browning, Barbara, 1961-
Title: A foreign sound / Barbara Browning.
Description: New York NY : Bloomsbury Academic, 2017. | Series: 33 1/3 Brazil | Includes bibliographical references and index.
Identifiers: LCCN 2017010645 (print) | LCCN 2017011717 (ebook) | ISBN 9781501319242 (ePDF) | ISBN 9781501319259 (ePUB) | ISBN 9781501319235 (pbk. : alk. paper)
Subjects: LCSH: Veloso, Caetano. Foreign sound. | Veloso, Caetano—Criticism and interpretation. | Popular music—United States—History and criticism. | Popular music—Brazil—History and criticism.
Classification: LCC ML420.V3276 (ebook) | LCC ML420.V3276 B76 2017 (print) |DDC 782.42164092—dc23
LC record available at https://lccn.loc.gov/2017010645

ISBN:	HB:	978-1-5013-1922-8
	PB:	978-1-5013-1923-5
	ePub:	978-1-5013-1925-9
	ePDF:	978-1-5013-1924-2

Series: 33 ⅓ Brazil

Cover image © 333sound

Typeset in the UK by Fakenham Prepress Solutions, Fakenham, Norfolk NR21 8NN
Printed and bound in the United States of America

Contents

Acknowledgments

My sincere thanks to Jason Stanyek for the invitation to write this book, to the anonymous readers of the original proposal, and to Bloomsbury for taking it on. Arto Lindsay was, as ever, extraordinarily generous in offering his encouragement and insights. Of course my greatest debt is to Caetano—for saying he liked the idea of the book, for reading the manuscript and offering corrections, but most of all, for making these strange, foreign sounds.

Introduction

What is a Foreign Sound?

Don't fear if you hear
A foreign sound to your ear ...
BOB DYLAN, "ITS ALRIGHT MA (I'M ONLY BLEEDING)"

Caetano Veloso recorded his brilliant and idiosyncratic American songbook album in 2004—but it wasn't his first album in English.[1] That, in fact, was his 1971 eponymous third album, recorded in England during the period of his exile from the military dictatorship.[2] There, and in many of the songs across the span of his career, Caetano[3] has probed the questions implicit in the title of *A Foreign Sound*: What makes a song sound foreign? What makes it sound "American,"[4] or Brazilian?

At the time of *A Foreign Sound*'s release, Caetano wrote a text recounting the genesis of the project. As early as the period of his exile, he'd considered recording an "Anglo-American" repertoire upon his return to Brazil, but that didn't happen. In the mid-'90s, long after having given up entirely on the idea, he was visiting New York when Bob Hurwitz, the president of Nonesuch, tried to resuscitate it. "Bob insisted, he said that I was the only person in the world who could record Cole Porter and Bob Dylan on the same CD."[5] The prospect stoked something in his imagination—on the plane back to

Brazil he fantasized about a version of Dylan's "It's Alright Ma" accompanied by a cello playing Dylan's guitar part, which sounded so much to him like a fragment of the soundtrack of the film *Deus e o Diabo na Terra do Sol* by the great Brazilian avant-garde director Glauber Rocha—but the plan remained on the back burner as he went on to compose three other albums of originals, and record an additional live version of the last, as well as a collaborative album with Jorge Mautner.[6] Finally, after a gap of nearly ten years, he came back to the project. Even then, he said, the process of putting the album together was somewhat rankling: he kept thinking of other things he'd rather be doing. By that time, it had become a little predictable for a singer of his age to take a turn at interpreting North American standards.[7] He describes his own take on the American songbook as "atypical," mixing a range of styles and periods of composition that was sure to alienate practically everyone. "Maybe my recordings will arouse some skewed interest," he wrote. "I don't hope for more than that."

Skewed or not, the recordings are more than interesting—in fact, they are deeply illuminating, perplexing, and often gorgeous. But some U.S. listeners were ill-prepared to hear just how much was going on in them. *A Foreign Sound* was evidently addressed to an English-speaking audience, but not everyone seemed to apprehend just how loving and yet also how aggressive it was as an address. To understand all that, perhaps one needs to know something about Caetano's long-standing preoccupation with the global hegemony of U.S. popular culture, and also what constitutes the Brazilian sound. These are issues taken up explicitly in his 1997 memoir,

Tropical Truth,[8] but they are also embedded in his entire discography.

Caetano once told me that, after the album was recorded, Bob Hurwitz said to him, "It's a fucking masterpiece." But then he added, in what Caetano understood as a gentle tone of consolation, that it was a "Brazilian" album. I'm not sure if that was the tone that Hurwitz intended, or what it might mean, from his perspective, to say that the album was "Brazilian." Caetano seemed to think it meant that a U.S. listenership wouldn't be so interested. In fact, much of the response by U.S. critics and listeners was positive, but there did seem to be some confusion about his motivation in recording these songs, and also about the political implications of his doing so. Stephen M. Deusner's review in *Pitchfork* began, "Whenever a non-English-speaking musician makes his or her English-language debut [*sic*], there's always a suggestion that it's a commercially motivated attempt to reach a larger audience. More importantly, if that record is a cover album of American standards, the endeavor unavoidably becomes a political statement."[9] Deusner leaves it an open question what kind of "statement" the album might be making, noting that it could be read as "an act of appropriation, a kind of reverse musical imperialism," but also saying that it "plays like an eloquent defense of" the global hegemony of U.S. popular music, resulting "in what could be considered an act of diplomacy." (John Bush's review for *AllMusic* similarly used a diplomatic figure, calling Caetano "the statesman of Brazilian pop."[10])

Deusner's review cites only the last three sentences from the liner notes, saying that Caetano "writes somewhat apologetically: 'People all over the world would like to find a way of thanking American popular music for having made their lives and their music richer and more beautiful. Many try. So do I.'" But these lines follow a stunning pastiche of both original and appropriated text that is utterly cacophonic—and often entirely the opposite of "apologetic." To say these liner notes are "ambiguous" would give the wrong impression. They are simultaneously utterly scathing and loving, both in full measure. The vituperative comments include citations of one U.S. artist denigrating his compatriot musicians (Frank Sinatra calls rock "the most brutal, ugly, desperate, vicious form of expression it has been my misfortune to hear"), and Caetano himself trashing Nirvana ("Ivan Lins is music. Nirvana is rubbish")—despite the fact that his cover of "Come as You Are" is one of the most meticulously, sensitively rendered tracks on this album. There's a cryptic but suggestive reference from Bob Dylan to the music of Brazil ("an' people perhaps like a soft Brazilian singer ... I have given up at making any attempt at perfection"[11]). Caetano also cites a character from the feature-length film he wrote and directed in 1986, *O Cinema Falado* (The Talkies): "The English language is an important subject for those who want to dominate music because it is the language of domination. I want to dominate music. My master wants to dominate dominion itself. I'll teach music to him." It's a paraphrase, an inversion and an extension of Caliban, of course. "You taught me language, and my profit on't / Is, I know how to curse."

Shamelessness

… sua vergonha tão graciosa …[12]

PERO VAZ DE CAMINHA

I first encountered Caetano's music as a foreign exchange student in Brazil in 1978, when I was sixteen years old. The shock of that encounter had to do with a sense of strangeness, but also of familiarity and recognition. That encounter was as much about estranging me from my own fixed sense of national identity as it was about familiarizing me with a foreign sound.

When I applied to the American Field Service, they didn't ask me what country I wanted to go to. I had some vague fantasy of ending up in France or Switzerland—I'd been studying French at school—but I was assigned to Bauru, São Paulo. Bauru is about two hundred miles inland from the state capital. It's a railroad hub. There are a couple of universities there, including a USP campus specializing in dentistry. There's a classic sandwich named after the town, which entails roast beef, melted cheese, and pickles on a roll. There's also a great song by the belated Brazilian rocker, Cazuza, called "A Garota de Bauru," the girl from Bauru.[13] It's about an unapologetic slut who's managing to survive in an environment of stultifying small-mindedness.

Bauru is about the size of Pittsburgh, and, like that city, it's at a moderate remove from the country's biggest metropolis—actually a little closer to São Paulo than Pittsburgh is to New York. But if I were to say, roughly, "Bauru is the Pittsburgh of Brazil," what would that mean? What does it mean, anyway, to think that there might be a correspondence between an industrial, relatively populous city in the U.S. and another in Brazil? Why would I need to find a correspondence to give you a sense of the place? Would it give you any sense at all? And would it sound like I was disparaging both towns?

In truth, Bauru was for me, at sixteen, fairly charmed. I quickly made a best friend there. We went to the local discotheque and danced under flashing lights, which felt sexy. I had a little romance with my friend's bookish older brother, who tried valiantly (on the sly, as I was living with a family with ties to the military regime) to teach me something about leftist political resistance. That also felt sexy. Still, it was in the home of my politically conservative host family that I first heard a song written by Caetano Veloso, though not the version recorded by him.[14] It was a version recorded by the very palatable Quarteto em Cy,[15] a group of well-bred sisters from Ibirataia, Bahia: Cybele, Cylene, Cynara, and Cyva. The title of the song was "Love, Love, Love"—just like that, in English, though the rest of the lyric was in Portuguese—and in the affable girl-group harmonies of these sisters, it sounded innocent enough.

But when I actually listened to the words, I intuited, though I didn't really understand, that something very complicated was happening in them. They were dense and ambiguous, topical and playful, but also, I was pretty sure, sincere in their moments of both national utopianism and global ambition. And I was also pretty sure that my nation, my language, and I were implicated. Dictionary in hand, I translated the lyrics into my journal—and thus began a long process of learning the Portuguese language through popular songs—particularly Caetano's. That was also a process of coming to apprehend the country in which I found myself. "Absurd," the song went—"Brazil may be absurd …" But, it continued, Brazil had a musicality, a physicality of singular beauty, which it was casting out into the world, bathing in the tide of utopia—proliferating, ferocious, in the dense forest, in the swirling cosmos. Free, strong figures were coming into focus … And one of them was the figure to whom the song attributed its own repetitive refrain: "*Pelé disse*: Love, love, love." (Pelé said: Love, love, love.)

Indeed, the most revered soccer player of all time, Pelé, famously said "Love, love, love."[16] It was October 1, 1977, at the close of his farewell game, an exhibition match for a sold-out crowd at Giants Stadium, in which he played one half for his adopted team, the New York Cosmos, and one half for his old Brazilian team, Santos. And when it was over, he took a microphone and addressed his fans on both sides of the stadium, and far beyond it: "Say three times after me: Love! Love! Love!" Maybe it was a general call for something like transnational cooperations, modeled on the capacity of one man to play for two teams, but this farewell was also an imperative to recognize Pelé's astonishing popularity—to acknowledge that, while he was thoroughly Brazilian (in fact, he grew up in Bauru!), he was beloved around the world. But why did the world have to acknowledge his undeniable magnificence in English? Why did that spectacle of his transcendence need to take place in Giants Stadium—an arena consecrated to the specifically "American" form of "football" that would seem determined to exclude the understanding of that term across the rest of the planet?

Pelé wasn't the first ferociously talented and charismatic Brazilian to burst into global prominence, and he wasn't the first one to take his gifts to the U.S. He also wasn't the first one to be referenced in a song by Caetano. In 1967, Caetano penned "Tropicália," the "manifesto-song" that would also give name to an entire aesthetic movement,[17] which closes with the iconic figure who seemed to embody all the complexities of Brazilian performance for global export: "*Carmen Miranda-da-da-da-da*." In fact, each verse of the song, a work of caustic social critique, concludes with a seemingly exultant refrain pairing two dissonant figures from Brazilian popular culture (in this final strophe, the larger-than-life '40s star is conjoined with "A Banda," a famous song by Caetano's *engagé* contemporary, Chico Buarque), and each time, the unlikely pair trail off in the repetition of a final syllable. But the "*da-da-da-da*" of Carmen Miranda is itself a complex trail which Caetano would retrace years later in an essay commissioned by the *New York Times*, published with the title, "Caricature and Conqueror, Pride and Shame."[18] When the essay was published in Portuguese in the *Folha de São Paulo*, the title made more explicit at least one understanding of Carmen's trail: "*Carmen Miranda Dada*."[19] As the English title suggests, the essay is a meditation on what it means for a Brazilian artist—or for Brazilians generally—to consider the ways in which Brazil has been and can be represented on the global stage, and consumed in the global market.

Carmen was "a typical girl from Rio, born in Portugal, who, using a blatantly vulgar though elegant stylization of the clothes characteristic of a *baiana* [an Afro-descendant woman from Bahia], had conquered the world and become the highest-paid woman entertainer in the United States." The essay goes on to acknowledge her genuine musical and comedic virtuosity, but also the humiliation experienced by Brazilians in seeing their national identity caricatured so extravagantly. "Even today, to write these words about her is something painful and difficult for me." Her image, he says, continues to haunt every staging of Brazilian music in the U.S., even in collaborations among sophisticated artists. "Tom Zé's experimental sambas released by David Byrne, Naná Vasconcelos and Egberto Gismonti … She is always present. Airto shaking traditional Brazilian trinkets in Miles Davis's band in 1971. Flora Purim and Chick Corea." The specter remains. But the essay ends poignantly, referencing a famous photograph captured in a photo shoot with Cesar Romero, when Carmen Miranda's skirt suddenly swooshed up, accidentally exposing her naked pudendum. Caetano explains that he first saw that scandalous photo in 1971, when he was in London, and it made him think of the Portuguese colonist Pêro Vaz de Caminha's letter to King Manuel I (1500),[20] which speaks rapturously, if somewhat playfully, of the exposed "shames"—*vergonhas*, a Portuguese euphemism for genitalia—of the indigenous women, of which, ironically, they seem to have no shame. "I thought it particularly significant that our representative should have been the only one among all the figures of the Olympus of Hollywood to show her 'shame' and that she should have done it inadvertently, innocently … In the arms of Cesar Romero, with a pure Hollywood smile on her lips, surrounded by glitter full of intention and control, everything about and around her seemed obscene next to the innocence of her sex."

All of the contrivances, all of the artificiality attached to the machine of global popular culture, were what constituted "Carmen Miranda," but her blameless, exposed part was pure Dada. Caetano's essay—characteristic of his prose in both its acuity and its lyricism—sparked the interest of a U.S. publisher, leading to an invitation to write the book-length manuscript that would eventually become *Tropical Truth*. The meditation on Carmen Miranda opened out onto a larger consideration of what provoked the Tropicália movement, and what relationship it bore to other artistic movements, including Dada, with its explicit critique of commercialism, but also Pop Art, with its apparent embrace of the same. But of course that's a reductive account of both Dada and Pop Art. Caetano once told a journalist, "When I put [Carmen Miranda] in [my] song, it was like Andy Warhol putting the soup can in his painting."[21] Like Warhol's citations of both pop stars and products, Caetano's glance at Carmen, with its glimpse of her private part, constituted neither pure parody nor adulation, but something like wordless awe.

Is it necessary to point out that in meditating on the conundrum of the Brazilian pop icon in a global market, Caetano was already, in the late '60s, coming to terms with his own future trajectory? The term "global market" perhaps overemphasizes the financial aspect of this question. But indeed the two reviews of *A Foreign Sound* that I've already cited open, almost identically, with the specter of capitulation to capital. There's Deusner's "suggestion [see above] that it's a commercially motivated attempt to reach a larger audience." And there's this, just slightly subtler, from Bush: "When an international artist records an English-language album, crossover is usually in the cards." In his press release for *A Foreign Sound*, Caetano doesn't deny a consideration of the market, but says that's not exactly what interested him: "When I made *Fina estampa* (1995), I was already thinking about the question of moving into an area of greater power, which is the Spanish language. The Portuguese language is a ghetto: although there are many speakers in the Portuguese world, very few understand it outside of that world. English implies much more power than Spanish. It may look like I want to expand the market, enter into the big world! I have even greater ambitions than that, but not exactly that."[22] The point, in a way, is that the "greater ambitions" have something to do with forcing us—all of us—to understand that part of the "domination" exerted by U.S. popular culture has to do with never letting anyone forget about the "market" as a sign of cultural validation.

But working in a foreign language has ramifications that go far beyond marketability. And if he has described Portuguese as a "ghetto," he's also expressed his commitment to it. During his period of exile in London, Caetano sent a number of short pieces to *O Pasquim*, a left-wing publication in Brazil that often featured humorous but also politically trenchant reflections on the historical moment. In one, he addressed his attitude to recording in English. He told the comical story of the composition of the sleeve notes for his debut solo album (the one containing "Tropicália"), before he'd left Brazil. He said he'd misplaced the text he'd originally written for the album cover, and found himself with Fernando Lobo at a production meeting in a restaurant having to quickly reproduce, longhand, the notes he'd originally prepared:

> While I was at work [trying to reconstruct the lost text], people were talking all around me, even *to* me. "I would like to make," I struggled to remember, "a protest song of esteem and consideration, but this Portuguese language makes me crazy [*louco*]"—that's what I wrote, and I immediately perceived that I hadn't written *hoarse* [*rouco*] as in the earlier version. I scratched out "crazy" and wrote "hoarse" instead. I don't know if that's what gave Fernando the idea to reproduce my manuscript on the back of the record, or if he'd already spoken of this idea before. I just know that I agreed to this idea so as not to complicate things … Anyway, I liked the joke. Not so much the joke that came out of the error, but the original joke. Just because to say that the Portuguese language made me hoarse was the truth, while to say that it made me crazy gave the impression that once again I was emphasizing the fact that we spoke and wrote in a non-exportable language. When, in truth, I wasn't feeling that at all. On the contrary: I was really happy, composing shamelessly, with no dream of exportation.[23]

The shamelessness of that state of innocence, "with no dream of exportation," of course resounds in that anecdote he'd tell years later of encountering Carmen Miranda's shameless private part.

In the 1970 essay in *O Pasquim*, just two years after the carefree moment of innocence, and now writing songs in English, Caetano said that in retrospect the whole story struck him as funny. Now, in fact, the question of language was entirely different. It was the "English language [that made him] crazy. Simone Weil wrote that, for a believer, it's as dangerous to switch religions as it is for a writer to switch languages." But with a characteristic shift from this lofty, erudite suggestion to one of self-effacement, he concluded, "This has nothing to do with me because I'm not a writer: I'm a radio singer."

Of course, Caetano *is* a writer, and he already was a lyricist of astonishing originality when he made that disavowal. But I wouldn't call it a case of false modesty. If I said the liner notes of *A Foreign Sound* are not so much ambiguous or ambivalent as they are utterly scathing and loving, both in full measure, I'd say the grandiosity (more than one critic has preferred the term "pretentiousness"[24]) and modesty embedded in many of Caetano's public pronouncements about his own work are both honest, and in full force.

The Voice

Melhor do que isso só mesmo o silêncio.
Melhor do que o silêncio só João.[25]

CAETANO VELOSO, "PRA NINGUÉM"

So what about that claim to being a "radio singer"? Well, that he also undeniably was. He was a full-fledged pop star when he left Brazil in 1969, if a controversial one.[26] It should, by now, be clear that the notion of a pop star is, was, has always been, a conceptual figure of interest to Caetano, and one with political ramifications. He's certainly not the only pop star to have explicitly pondered those ramifications.[27] But the phrase "radio singer"—*cantor de rádio*—puts a different emphasis on things. It's simultaneously a more diminutive position, implying one's imbrication in the banal promotional structures of mass culture, but also an evocative one, calling our attention to the very sound of the voice that becomes a part of the ambient soundscape of popular life.[28] I've been focussing on language, and some of the lyrical preoccupations that characterize Caetano's music, but there's much to be said as well about vocal quality and style.

When I told Caetano's friend and sometime collaborator Arto Lindsay that I was going to write about *A Foreign Sound*, he said he liked the idea—it wasn't the most obvious album to write about, as the compositions weren't Caetano's own, but Arto called it "his most singerly record." He had some other interesting perceptions, which I'll say more about below, but I was struck by that comment about the focus in the album on vocal performance. In fact, I'm not sure I think it's his most singerly record—although that would seem to make sense, given that his contribution is primarily one of vocal interpretation (though he co-arranged most of the tracks and also plays guitar on many). But his singerly explorations—whether through explicit[29] extended technique, the referencing of vocal styles not typically associated with popular music, the evocation of the sounds of other singers, including the most mellifluous of crooners, or the exploration of the specificity of the grain[30] of his own "natural" voice—have been present throughout his career. (To tell the truth, in my opinion one of his most affecting albums, at the level of vocal performance, is *Omaggio a Federico e Giulietta*, a live concert recorded in Rimini, Italy, during which he was suffering from laryngitis[31]—which is to say, I'm not sure that the "hoarseness" that either one's own or a foreign language presents one is necessarily a bad thing. Nor perhaps is the "craziness.")

For many people outside of Brazil, the mere mention of Caetano's name evokes the ethereal falsetto of his version of "Cucurrucucú Paloma" in Pedro Almadóvar's 2002 film, *Hable con ella* (Talk to Her).[32] The sensitivity of that performance is, of course, heightened by the way in which it's framed in the film (a small chamber performance brings the singer's spectators to tears), and it's certainly true that, in his extreme upper register, he's capable of rendering literally breathtaking fragility. But he's often experimented with other vocal capacities, including the depths of his baritone. One of the most remarkable songs on his most recent album, *Abraçaço*, "Estou triste," (I'm Sad) is sung first in his baritone range, and then an octave up in his tremulous falsetto—but it's the low range that seems to be the very *voice* of sadness. Still, strangely, it's difficult to perceive just how low is that song, or many of the songs recorded in his lower register, unless you try to sing along. There's a quality to his voice that I once read described as "silvery,"[33] and indeed, it's often even mercurial—*quicksilver*—which can give the impression of his singing higher than in fact he is. He's nearly always referred to as a tenor (John Bush's review, cited above, calls him a "high tenor"), though his range goes much lower.

In regard to the question of extended technique or moments of intentionally jarring vocal performance, Lorraine Leu has suggested that the early part of Caetano's career was a period of particularly intense experimentation, and that this pushing of the envelope of vocal style was perhaps a response to the restrictions of political censorship.[34] If lyrics had external constraints, perhaps singerly choices could make audible the subversive or countercultural impulse that had to be coded or understated in the words. But Leu also follows Brazilian critic Luiz Tatit in suggesting that Caetano was simultaneously searching for a new *canção de radio* sound: an unapologetically popular voice taking inspiration from a broad range of commercially successful singers, from Brazil and beyond.[35] Which is a compressed way of saying that, even at the level of vocal style, he was working through the same impulses of iconoclasm and iconophilia that characterized his lyrics. To my mind, some of the singerly choices on *A Foreign Sound* reflect on a long trajectory of searching for the proper voice of the (mere?) "radio singer" he once claimed to be. Still, I'd argue that *A Foreign Sound* is a meta-singerly album—that is, the vocal aesthetics are self-reflexive in the same way that the choices of repertoire are, commenting on a long-established preoccupation in his discography. This doesn't mean that the choices aren't aesthetically or affectively powerful, but that they're highly intentional.

On the iconoclastic side, some of Caetano's early vocal experimentation bore a certain resemblance to the literary experimentation of the Brazilian concrete poets, Augusto and Haroldo de Campos, and Décio Pignatari, who had similarly evidenced an interest in recuperating the signs of popular culture and advertising as material for artistic production.[36] The *concretistas*, though of an older generation, embraced the *tropicalistas* enthusiastically. But the materiality of language for these poets operated most obviously on the visual plane, whereas for the *tropicalistas* it served as sonic matter. The material of quotidian language *in the mouth* presented not merely a political issue to masticate (including the prevalence of foreign sounds, like "baby, baby" and "yeah, yeah, yeah"), but also, quite literally, *sound to chew on*. Diction could be materially interesting in itself.[37] But there were other vocal traditions that provided other ways of exploring language's materiality—notably the vocal styles of northeastern trouba-dours whose Arab-influenced inflections can be traced to medieval Iberian traditions. This vocal tradition also includes peculiarities in diction that extend even further the notion of language as something to be chewed and swallowed—a vocal effect employed, for example, at the end of his 1971 recording of "Maria Bethânia." Moments in which Caetano inserts such culturally specific—and surely, to a non-Brazilian audience, alien-sounding—vocal techniques into an album of English-language songs might be read as an intentional affront to his Anglophone listeners, or as a melancholy harkening back home in the midst of a love song[38] to foreigners. Or it could be both. In *A Foreign Sound*, many of the moments of vocal affront are, on the contrary, ones in which he's reflecting back some of the peculiarities of various strains of Anglo-American popular music.

But he's also long been in conversation with vocalists of unalloyed beauty. One is his lifelong friend and collaborator, Gilberto Gil. As I mentioned, I first encountered Caetano's music in the '70s. In 1983, I returned to Brazil, having graduated from college and landed a Fulbright grant to study popular poetry. I inherited from a previous Fulbright grantee a quiet little apartment in the Barra neighborhood of Salvador, Bahia. Although Caetano's main residence then—as now—was in Rio, he was born in the state of Bahia, studied in Salvador, and he's also kept a home there for most of his life. In the early '80s I found it striking that many people, particularly the other expats I met in Bahia, seemed compelled to "choose" between Caetano's music and that of his fellow *tropicalista* Gil, who was also from Bahia, and who had been exiled with Caetano in London. "Which one do you like?", people would ask, as though this were an obvious question. (Comparisons were also unavoidably drawn to Caetano's sister, Maria Bethânia—hailed in that '71 song which takes her name as its title—who though four years younger emerged very early as the more obviously gifted singer of the family;[39] Caetano has always acknowledged this as self-evident.) Both Caetano and Gil have always been extremely deferential to one another, and when they perform together today, they're most typically described as "complementing" one another's style.[40] If one were to characterize Gil's voice in relation to a substance, as I have with Caetano's quicksilver quality, the most obvious one would be honey—warm, thick, dense. I confess that in the early '80s, I found the grain of Gil's voice, at this purely elemental level, the more pleasurable one—but Caetano's songwriting seemed to me entirely singular.[41] It took me some time to be sensitive to the ways in which his voice was rubbing up against his language.[42]

But in the early '80s—and ever after—the singer I listened to most religiously[43] was the one with the most granular voice of all,[44] the voice that seemed to me to embody everything Barthes had attempted to articulate about the voice's potential to conjoin signification and physicality: João Gilberto. Caetano himself has often said that hearing his music was what led him to pursue music himself, and in *Tropical Truth* there are numerous references to João Gilberto's innovations and brilliance—even his "poetry,"[45] though he is known as an interpreter rather than a composer. Caetano doesn't dwell on the question that seems to me most pressing—the shocking sense of intimacy that João Gilberto's voice creates.[46] He does, however, talk about what João Gilberto took from—and rejected in—the popular singers that preceded him. And he's repeatedly argued that João Gilberto's musical innovations were a jolt on many levels.[47]

A very simplistic account would tell you this: in or around 1957, João Gilberto developed a highly distilled sound combining a minimalist, syncopated guitar technique capturing the essence of polyrhythmic percussive samba, and a hushed, vibratoless vocal style that added another layer of rhythmic complexity by sometimes rushing ahead of and sometimes dragging behind the beat. That description does little to express the effect he created. Ruy Castro calls João's 1958 recording of "Chega de Saudade" "one minute and fifty-nine seconds that changed everything."[48] Bossa nova—the "new style"—became not merely an interpretive style, but an aesthetic basis for composition, most famously by João's collaborator Antonio Carlos Jobim (co-author with Vinícius de Moraes of "Chega de Saudade"). But João also interpreted traditional sambas, as well as the works of a prior generation of Brazilian crooners, like Orlando Silva, the so-called "singer of the multitudes," an enormously popular recording star of the '30s and '40s.[49] And João also recorded standards from the American Songbook—inevitably provoking some of the same questions that frame *A Foreign Sound*. But when João sang Cole Porter or the Gershwin brothers, they sounded tailor-made for bossa nova. It was an entirely different proposition. For João, interpreting a classic repertoire—whether of Brazilian sambas or U.S. standards—was a way to simultaneously acknowledge how those musical vocabularies had formed him, but also to completely subvert them in a style which was his own. *A Foreign Sound* takes the conversation of national sounds to another degree of complexity.

To Croon

If you don't know the guy on the other side of the world, love him anyway because he's just like you … It's one world, pal.

FRANK SINATRA, *PLAYBOY* INTERVIEW

All this is to say that, despite their mutual interest in creating something new, neither João nor Caetano has ever held disdain for the "radio singers" that preceded them, in Brazil or beyond. On the contrary. Of course, as all this came to pass, U.S. artists were also listening to Brazilian music. To say that Chet Baker and cool jazz broadly speaking left a clear mark on João's style would be radically reductive: the influence was running in both directions. João's recordings with Stan Getz were watershed moments in the history of jazz, and in the 1960s (as I'll discuss below), bossa nova compositions constituted an enormous proportion of new "jazz standards." It doesn't even seem particularly jarring to see "The Girl from Ipanema" included in conversations about the "Great American Songbook."

And Frank Sinatra, the emblematic U.S. crooner, had an intense, though apparently self-conscious, engagement with bossa nova, and with the style's preeminent composer. *Francis Albert Sinatra & Antônio Carlos Jobim* was recorded in 1967. The title of the album almost seems like a strange capitulation on Sinatra's part to Jobim's professional use of his full name—why not *Frank Sinatra & Tom Jobim*? Anyway, the parallel pairing of the two musical giants carried over into a second album, titled more simply *Sinatra-Jobim*, which was released as an 8-track tape in 1970. Sinatra ended up pulling the project as a record release, although he included some tracks on his 1971 *Sinatra & Company* album and on a later Jobim sessions compilation. (In 2010, Concord Records would go ahead and issue the complete set of Sinatra-Jobim sessions.) What might have led Sinatra to hold some of the recordings back? The '67 album was nominated for the Grammy Award for Album of the Year (Sinatra had won the two prior years), but lost to The Beatles' *Sgt. Pepper's Lonely Hearts Club Band*. That surely says more about the achievements of that album and the global embrace of the musical idiom that Sinatra would call (not specifically in reference to The Beatles, of course) "the most brutal, ugly, desperate, vicious form of expression it has been my misfortune to hear." But might the "chairman of the board," the reigning voice of "American" song, have balked at the challenge of interpreting a foreign sound?

He was already deeply imbricated in that sound, in fact. And it wasn't only Jobim, the crossover Brazilian composer of jazz standards, who had been studying him. Caetano—an artist who has much more typically been likened to Anglo-American artists in the vein of rock 'n' roll[50]—was listening as well. Recently, on the centenary of Sinatra's birth, the *New York Times* asked Caetano, Iggy Pop, and Kurt Elling to recall moments of hearing Sinatra that had marked them. Caetano said:

I was 18. [If you do the math, this would be 1960: Caetano was born in 1942.] In my tiny Bahia house, I would spend hours listening to the album "Close to You." "It's Easy to Remember,"

"Everything Happens to Me," "With Every Breath I Take," "P.S. I Love You" … Sinatra at his soberest, most dignified manliness. His natural musicianship in perfect calm. Nelson Riddle. That album formed my taste. I loved Ray Charles, Monk and Miles. And listened to João Gilberto more than anything. But Sinatra's "Close to You" played a special role in my musical life.[51]

Close to You was recorded in 1957—the same year that João was formulating his signature sound—and it's an unusually sparse and delicate record in the Sinatra discography. In fact, the only other recordings by Sinatra that critics find vaguely similar are the ones he'd do with Jobim a decade later. And though Sinatra's own vocal choices on *Close to You* obviously weren't influenced by João's, it's perhaps not surprising that Caetano gravitated to this particular album. Its trace is completely audible on *A Foreign Sound*—including in the arrangements. In fact, writing of the album in the *Village Voice*, Robert Christgau called Jaques Morelenbaum, Caetano's co-arranger, "a salty Nelson Riddle."[52] I'll say more about the "saltiness" of some of the arrangements below, but the comparison between Morelenbaum's elegant chamber orchestrations and Riddle's—particularly on *Close to You*—is perfectly apt.

And the singing? Much has been written about what makes Sinatra's singing distinctive. To my own ear, it's less a question of the grain of his voice than his capacity to foreground the story of a song—in truth, I've always appreciated him more as an actor than a singer—even when he's ostensibly singing,

not acting. But I can't say that this is the quality I hear rever-
berating in *A Foreign Sound*. There's perhaps a kind of narrative
running through the album, but if you call it that, you'd have
to qualify it as a kind of postmodern meta-narrative.[53] I'm
tempted, rather, to follow the trail that Caetano himself gives
us in his account of the mark that Sinatra left on him: "natural
musicianship in perfect calm," "sober … dignified manliness."
All of these notions—nature, calm, dignity, and perhaps most
of all manliness—are abundantly present on *A Foreign Sound*.
But they're somewhat (to use Caetano's term) skewed in his
interpretation of them.

To Cannibalize

*La plus grande vengeance dont les sauvages usent, et qui
leur semble la plus cruelle et indigne, est de manger leur
ennemi.*[54]

ANDRÉ THEVET, *LES SINGULARITÉS DE LA FRANCE ANTARCTIQUE*

In 1988, I went back to Bahia to finish writing my dissertation,
which was about French ethnographic writing on Brazil.
In the course of conducting my research, I'd spent some
time in France, but I figured that for the last few months of
writing I could stretch my fellowship funds a little further in
Brazil. It wasn't really necessary to complete my study, but
I missed Bahia, and I felt like it was the right place to bring
my writing to a close. I installed myself in a little rented
lean-to on "Mermaid Hill"—a small promontory sticking into

the bay in the neighborhood of Rio Vermelho. Some years later, Caetano would come to own a home on the upscale opposite side of our little hill. That side had a long, paved drive that led up to a security gate. Our side was decidedly more rustic. Nobody had a car. To get to the houses, you had to climb up some steep, dilapidated concrete steps. The residences were mostly precarious constructions with jerry-rigged electrical wiring and dubious plumbing. But even on our side, the hill had one great advantage: it was practically the only spot in Salvador where you weren't separated from the ocean by an avenue. At night, you just heard the crashing of the waves.[55] The view from my small square window was just the shimmering surface of the water, and, at night, the twinkling lights on the island of Itaparica. The distant electric lights looked like stars, as though the horizon had been flipped.

My dissertation began with an analysis of sixteenth-century accounts of the short-lived effort to establish a French colony in Guanabara Bay, in what is today Rio de Janeiro, and worked its way to the writings of the seminal twentieth-century anthropologist, Claude Lévi-Strauss. That early, doomed colony, first described in detail by the Franciscan priest André Thevet, was called "*La France Antarctique*"—with "Antarctic" obviously not signifying our understanding of that term today, but rather, "on the other side of the world." Thevet's descriptions of indigenous Brazilians cast them as oddly familiar and yet inverted versions of the French. What interested me was this notion of a kind of upside-down world (Australia and New Zealand were similarly configured as the "antipodes" of the northern hemisphere)—as configured by the colonists. These kinds of configuration of inversion in the southern hemisphere have been invoked at various historical moments both to justify and to decry the violences of imperialism. (The sympathetic invocations might be read as elaborations of Frank Sinatra's mild proposition regarding the guy on the flipside of the planet: "he's just like you … It's one world, pal.") I was interested in the continuity of the figure, despite the radically different arguments in the service of which it was deployed.

But upside-downness isn't the only significant figure in that history. Perhaps the even more relevant figure is one of the consumption of difference. Here's a radical simplification of its trail: André Thevet's cannibalizing "savages," cited above, were taken up by Montaigne in his great essay, "Des Cannibales," which was in turn taken up by Shakespeare in *The Tempest* in the figure of Caliban, who has often been read as the resistant colonial subject, and, as I've already suggested, hovers over any consideration not only of the shifting map of empire five hundred years ago, but also of the very question language, sound, and cultural imperialism with which we began. And again, to radically compress and simplify a major strain running through any discussion of what might constitute a specifically Brazilian aesthetic strategy: the notion of cannibalism was taken up by Brazilian intellectuals in the 1920s, notably Oswald de Andrade, who proposed, with Tarsila do Amaral in the *Manifesto Antropófago*, the "cultural devouring of imported techniques to re-elaborate them with autonomy, converting them into a product for export." And, as Caetano would write in *Tropical Truth*, "[Andrade's] idea of cultural cannibalism fit *tropicalistas* like a glove."[56]

If "Love, Love, Love" had been my entry point for thinking about this complicated terrain, Lévi-Strauss's *Tristes Tropiques* had become a kind of guidebook for navigating it. I don't mean it became a guidebook to my encounter with Brazil—far from it. I mean it became a guidebook to my encounter with my own foreignness in relation to Brazil. It's a book rife with self-estrangement. It made me feel very strange.

The year I was completing my dissertation was the year Caetano was recording an album that, in my mind, is deeply connected to *A Foreign Sound*. The name of the album is *Estrangeiro*. Foreign. And it opens with the song, "O Estrangeiro" ("The Foreigner/Stranger"), which could have served as the epigraph of the text I was writing. Except that it hadn't yet been recorded. The lyric ponders the various perspectives foreigners have had on Guanabara Bay—Paul Gauguin's rapture, Cole Porter's delight—but also Claude Lévi-Strauss's revulsion at what looked to him like a toothless mouth. "*E eu*," Caetano asks, "*menos a conhecera mais a amara? … O que é uma coisa bela?*" (And I, if I knew her less, would I love her more? … What is a beautiful thing?) Can one see one's own city with real clarity, or would that require the eyes of a stranger?

Anyone who's been to Rio de Janeiro would have to concede that there are certain undeniably exquisite views of the city. It's a mix of those famous, uncanny land forma-tions, lush, tropical vegetation, and the star-like lights of dense urbanity—a metropolis of surreality and extraordinary elegance. If one speaks of the ugliness of Rio's extreme economic disparity (with luxury high-rises abutting the brutally policed favelas), one is right, of course, but one isn't really denying the *physical* beauty of the city. At night, the favelas also sparkle like golden constellations.

This is the passage from *Tristes Tropiques* that Caetano references in "O Estrangeiro":

> It seems to me that the landscape in which Rio is set is out of proportion to its own dimensions. The Sugar Loaf Mountain, the Corcovado and the much-praised natural features appear to the traveler entering the bay like stumps sticking up here and there in a toothless mouth. Since these eminences are almost always swathed in a thick tropical mist, they seem totally unable to fill the horizon, for which in any case they would be inadequate. If you want a satisfactory view you must look at the bay from the landward side and look down upon it from the heights. On the seaward side, the optical illusion is the opposite of the one which obtains in New York; here, it is nature which has the appearance of an unfinished building-site.[57]

It's an unusual—in fact maybe a unique—perspective on Guanabara Bay. But I'm writing these words, now, from New York—the storied concrete jungle—and from my window here, I watch an enormous crane that has, for months now, been my constant reminder of the unfinished and unfinishable business of "rebuilding" lower Manhattan. If I recognize something in Lévi-Strauss's depiction of Guanabara Bay, it's the weird, inverted image of my own city and my own country, with its ethos of unrelenting development. Swallow this, or be eaten.

But my savage city is beautiful too. If I knew her less would I love her more? What is a beautiful thing? What is her foreign sound?

Notes

1 The Nonesuch website calls *A Foreign Sound* Caetano's "first album sung entirely in English," which is technically true, since the fourth track of his '71 album concludes with a refrain from a popular *cântico* of capoeira, and the last track is a cover of Luiz Gonzaga's classic northeastern *baião*, "Asa Branca." But the main lyrics on all of the original tracks were written and recorded in English. His 1969 album (also eponymous, alternatively known as the Álbum Branco) has two original songs in English. Five of the seven tracks on his 1972 *Transa* are in English. His 1975 *Qualquer Coisa* includes three Beatles covers, and there's another on his 1975 *Jóia*. *Velô* (1984) has two original songs in English (one previously recorded). His 1986 eponymous album includes songs by Michael Jackson, the Beatles, and Cole Porter. *Tropicália 2* with Gilberto Gil (1993) has a Hendrix cover. *Livro* (1986) includes a song in English by his son, Moreno.

2 The authoritarian régime had assumed power in a 1964 coup d'état, when Caetano was twenty-one years old. He and his collaborator and friend Gilberto Gil were imprisoned for two months in 1969, then placed under house arrest, and soon after they went into exile in London, where they remained until 1972. See Caetano Veloso, *Tropical Truth: A Story of Music and Revolution in Brazil*, trans. Isabel de Sena (Da Capo Press, Cambridge, MA, 2002), 218–68.

3 I hesitated over the choice to refer to Caetano by his first or last name in this book. Brazilian convention leans toward the former, but in the U.S. such familiarity might read as a lack of deference. That's certainly not my intention. But as I hope will become clear in the course of this book, the sense of familiarity—indeed intimacy—established between the popular singer and his listeners—as well as the moments of estrangement between them—are important aspects of this album, and of Caetano's entire musical trajectory.

4 I place the word "American" in inverted commas because, while many U.S. speakers use it in reference to their own nationality, plenty of citizens of the rest of the Americas find this an assumption of U.S. privilege, since they are also (North, Central, or South) Americans. I will, however, continue to refer to the "American songbook" because there are so many received ideas about the term, precisely the ones that this album presses us to reconsider in regard to both halves of it—that is, what is "American" music, and what are the "standards," "hits," or "classics" that should compose the songbook?

5 "Bob insistiu, disse que eu era a única pessoa do mundo que poderia gravar Cole Porter e Bob Dylan num mesmo CD." Caetano Veloso, "*A Foreign Sound* II," in *O mundo não é chato* (Companhia das Letras, São Paulo, 2005), 158, my translation above.

6 *Fina Estampa* (1994), *Livro* (1998), *Noites do Norte* (2000), *Noites do Norte ao Vivo* (2001), *Eu Não Peço Desculpa* (with Jorge Mautner, 2002).

7 The exemplary pop and rock artists who have recorded albums of standards are nearly all British, Ringo Starr anticipating the trend (*Sentimental Journey*, 1970). Bryan Ferry also recorded standards in the '70s, and went on to release his very successful *As Time Goes By* in 1999. Rod Stewart recorded *It Had to Be You* in 2002, and followed it with four additional "volumes" of standards. More recently, Paul McCartney released *Kisses on the Bottom* (2012), while Iggy Pop looked the other way across the Atlantic, mixing American standards with French ones (*Préliminaires*, 2009 and *Après*, 2012).

8 *Verdade Tropical* (Companhia das Letras, São Paulo, 1997), published in English as *Tropical Truth: A Story of Music and Revolution in Brazil*, tr. Isabel de Sena (Da Capo Press, Cambridge, MA, 2002).

9 http://pitchfork.com/reviews/albums/8429-a-foreign-sound/ (accessed 19 March 2017).

10 http://www.allmusic.com/album/a-foreign-sound-mw 0000329917 (accessed 19 March 2017).

11 Caetano had previously appropriated this very line, slightly modified, for a lyric of his own, placing it at the end of "O Estrangeiro," which I discuss below. When I first read the quotation, I had assumed that it was meant to be a sideways dig at "soft Brazilian music"—with "softness" suggesting a lack of political and/or aesthetic edge. But when I asked Caetano about it, he said that, "on the contrary, I've always instinctively felt the 'perfection' that appears in the next sentence referred (not really ironically) to João [Gilberto]." He told me to check Dylan's memoir, *Chronicles*, and indeed, in it he compares his own attempts to "break the rules" of popular song to the experiments of Brazilian musicians in the late '50s: "Latin artists were breaking rules, too. Artists like João Gilberto, Roberto Menescal and Carlos Lyra were breaking away from the drum infested samba stuff and creating a new form of Brazilian music with melodic changes. They were calling it bossa nova" (*Chronicles*, New York [Simon and Schuster, 2004], p. 67). I'll say much more about bossa's and Dylan's—as well as Caetano's—revolutionary impulses as I trace them through this album.

12 … her shame so graceful …

13 It's perhaps unnecessary to point out that the girl from Bauru was the (beautifully) vulgar analog to the seemly girl from Ipanema immortalized by Antonio Carlos Jobim.

14 Caetano's version was released on his 1978 album, *Muito* (Decca).

15 Quarteto em Cy's version was on their album of the same year, *Querelas do Brasil* (Philips).

16 You can watch the scene on multiple YouTube posts, and you can also find it on GIFs created, it seems, to perpetuate the moment ad infinitum. If the original cry demanded repetition, it seems that its immortalization in Caetano's lyric has helped to carry out the ferocious proliferation the song points to.

17 The name of the song was casually suggested, after its composition, by the cinematographer Luís Carlos Barreto, who perceived a kinship between the song and a work of that title by the artist Hélio Oiticica, and the name stuck (*Tropical Truth*, 119). The lyric is dizzying in its accumulation of images drawn from historical and literary texts, popular films, songs and television shows. It's been read astutely and minutiously by many critics. A number of these readings, including Caetano's own, are assembled and extended in Christopher Dunn's *Brutality Garden: Tropicália and the Emergence of a Brazilian Counterculture* (University of North Carolina Press, Chapel Hill, NC, 2001), 87–92.

18 Caetano Veloso, "Caricature and Conqueror, Pride and Shame," *New York Times*, October 20, 1991, H34.

19 Caetano also notes that the repeating syllable at the end recalled for him "Dadá, the *cangaceiro* [backlands bandit] Corisco's famous companion"—another clashing chord with both folkloric and avant-garde resonances. *Tropical Truth*, 118.

20 This letter is itself cited in the very opening of the recording of "Tropicália." In *Tropical Truth* (117), Caetano explains that in the recording studio the session drummer—who was as yet unaware of the subject matter of the lyric—heard the opening arrangement of percussion mixed with tropical birdsong, and was reminded of Pero Vaz's letter, which he playfully invoked, never imagining that his extemporaneous speech would be recorded and incorporated into the final arrangement of the song.

21 Quoted in Julian Dibbell, "Notes on Carmen," *The Village Voice* (29 October 1991). In *Tropical Truth*, Caetano elaborates: "In his portraits of both Marilyn and Elvis, I recognized at once that it was not the actress or the rock star that I was meant to be seeing but a visual image with a life of its own.

In Warhol's Marilyn I saw how raw images would become comments on the world if only we would abstain from commenting upon them." (18)

22 *O mundo não é chato*, 159.

23 *O mundo não é chato*, 315–16, my translation.

24 Lorraine Leu notes that many readers of Caetano's memoir found it a "pretentious attempt to intellectualise Tropicália," (Leu 146). Some have made the charge against some of his denser song lyrics, and he's sometimes concurred (particularly poignant to me is his concern around the tender, poetic song "Peter Gast" in *Sobre as letras*, 60). But the accusation of pretentiousness was surely most pronounced in the critical response to his feature-length film, *O Cinema Falado*—and this accusation he fully embraced, publishing an essay about the film titled—and declaring with a vengeance—"*Sou Pretencioso*" (I am pretentious; *O mundo não é chato*, 205–13).

25 "Better than this, only silence itself. Better than silence, only João." (It's interesting to note as well that while for Anglophone listeners the title of "Pra Ninguém" evokes the Beatles song that Caetano himself covered on *Qualquer Coisa*—"For No One"—for Brazilian listeners it evokes Chico Buarque's "Paratodos"—"For Everyone." Caetano acknowledges the link to Chico in the liner notes of *Livro*.

26 Public opinion at the time in Brazil of Caetano—and more broadly of the *tropicalista* musical movement—in relation to the work of their colleagues working in a more recognizably or narrowly "Brazilian" musical lineage (the exemplary figure being Chico Buarque) is a matter taken up not only in Caetano's memoir, but also in critical works by Gerard Béhague, Heloisa Buarque de Hollanda, Christopher Dunn, Lorraine Leu, Charles Perrone, and others.

27 It's tempting to say, for example, that David Bowie's entire career was a meta-commentary on that status.

28 I have distinct and very powerful sense memories of walking by, for example, an auto body repair shop on the Avenida Oceânica in Salvador, or through the tacky discount shopping area of the Baixa dos Sapateiros, and hearing Caetano's uncannily familiar voice straining out of the thumpy loudspeakers placed on the sidewalk outside, thus marking those locales indelibly.

29 Some would say audacious, or even, at times, intentionally jarring.

30 It perhaps goes without saying that I invoke here the grain of the voice as formulated by Roland Barthes, *Image— Music—Text*, trans. Stephen Heath (Hill and Wang, 1978), pp. 179–89.

31 "On the day that I finally arrived in Rimini to sing, my voice presented a kind of problem that until then I'd never experienced: deep in my larynx, something almost prevented me from emitting any sound at all, but the sounds that I managed to produce, uncomfortable but not exactly painful, came out considerably limpid. Such that my control of pitch and above all of intensity was exasperatingly limited. It was cold and humid in Rimini, but there was also an enormous emotion in me. This emotion involved sadness, an exalted pride, and vague fears linked to the meaning of my life." *Omaggio a Federico e Giulietta*, liner notes, my translation.

32 The song was written in 1954 by Tomás Méndez, and has been interpreted by many Latin artists, but Caetano's version has become a touchstone.

33 This, from an unattributed *New Yorker* "Goings on about Town" notice about an outdoor dance performance choreographed by Dean Moss in 2007: "In the background, Caetano Veloso's lilting, silvery voice wafts in and out, as in a dream." I was at that performance, and the description seemed to me exact. In fact, Caetano's voice was emanating from the small speakers of a portable boom box. Despite the minimalism of that apparatus, the sound was far from tinny. It was, precisely, and intensely, evocative of silver. http://www.newyorker.com/magazine/2007/09/03/dance-21 (accessed 19 March 2017).

34 Leu, 59–83.

35 Tatit, 275–6.

36 Caetano dedicates a chapter to them in *Tropical Truth* (132–48). Also, see Dunn (31–2).

37 The album on which he pushed this kind of experiment the furthest was his 1972 *Araçá Azul*, which, as everyone likes to point out, broke records (perhaps literally as well as figuratively) in the number of albums returned. (For the record: I love this album.)

38 Here, I don't refer to the specific song "Maria Bethânia" as a love song to foreigners, but rather to the album as a whole, which carries through it, as many great love songs do, a profound strain of ambivalence to the one(s) addressed.

39 Though less has been written about Maria Bethânia's artistic trajectory, the national (and regional) devotion to her is often of an order approaching idolatry. Indeed, beyond questions of natural power, timbre, or technique, she possesses a dramatic force that's perhaps without equal in Brazil. If one were to attempt to find a corresponding figure in U.S. popular music, the most obvious comparison (though not quite right) would be Nina Simone.

40 See, for example, Broughton: http://www.standard. co.uk/goingout/music/caetano-veloso-and-gilberto-gil-tour-review-they-complement-each-other-beautifully-10361269.html (accessed 19 March 2017).

41 As both a lyricist and a composer, Gil is himself extremely accomplished, and Brazilian popular song, generally speaking, is notoriously rich in both lyrical and musical achievement (see Castro, Dunn, McGowan and Pessanha, Murphy, Perrone, Vianna—and of course, Veloso).

42 To emphasize the physical and in fact erotic way in which the very flesh of the singer encounters language, I should perhaps say "the place where his tongue rubs up against his language," which is, precisely, the figure that Caetano himself used in the opening of the lyric of his song, "Língua" (*Velô*, 1984): "Gosto de sentir minha língua roçar a língua de Luís de Camões." (I like to feel my tongue rub up against the tongue/language of Luís de Camões.)

43 Of course I use the word figuratively, but some years later, when I got myself ordained for $15 on the Internet in the Church of Spiritual Humanism in order to be able to officiate at my brother's wedding, I only half-jokingly told friends that my particular denomination was the Church of

João Gilberto the Divine. Caetano has often defended his position as an atheist, while deferring respectfully to the various faiths (Catholic, Afro-Brazilian, and Evangelical) of his family members. But if he *were* to adhere to a religious doctrine, I think it would most obviously be that of my own tiny sect.

44 I don't even mean in the history of Brazilian popular music—I mean in the history of recorded music, of any genre, historical period or geographic location. This is, of course, a fanatical statement, but on this point I'd stand by my fanaticism. For years in the Department of Performance Studies at NYU, I'd introduce Barthes's writing on voice— as well as Wayne Koestenbaum's on operatic voice—by playing João Gilberto side by side with Maria Callas. While Koestenbaum takes one deep into the queen's ravaged throat, João Gilberto's voice seems to me the exemplary one that holds us in the erotic place of almost unbearable up-close exposure: one senses the hairs in his nose, the spit on his lips—even as one is brought into almost unbearably close contact with the language of the song. The sensitive microphone, of course, is part of this experience, but it's by no means reducible to a question of technology. The grain of his voice also comes into contact with that instrument in a very particular and remarkable way.

45 "I already considered João Gilberto a great poet, in every sense, because of the rhythm and the musical phrasing he could intertwine with the sounds and the meanings of the words he sang" (*Tropical Truth*, 87). João himself perhaps confirmed both Barthes's and Caetano's use of the writerly metaphors for vocal performance when he explained to a *New York Times* critic his need for a silent audience: "It is as if I'm writing on a blank piece of paper. It has to be very quiet for me to produce the sounds I'm thinking of" (John S. Wilson, "João Gilberto, Singer, Thrives in Understatement; Brazilian Guitarist Performs Bossa Nova Numbers at the Rainbow Grill," *New York Times*, October 15, 1968, 42).

46 Leu, also hyperbolically and yet, to my mind, entirely accurately, says that João Gilberto forged a style that "reinvent[ed] intimacy" (62).

47 This is a running theme throughout *Tropical Truth*—in fact, near the end of that book he laments that he didn't just write a book about João Gilberto instead of about himself—but for a compressed explanation of his influence, see the passage in which Caetano recounts not only his early musical enthusiasms but also the major philosophical, literary, artistic, and cinematic figures that formed him, concluding, "But every time, I always returned to my passion for João Gilberto to find a base and reestablish a perspective" (40–1).

48 Castro, 175.

49 Orlando Silva's defining feature, in terms of both vocal style and demeanor, was elegance. And despite the ways in which João Gilberto was forging a unique and in many ways challenging and disjunctive style some two decades later, to many U.S. listeners elegance remained his most audible quality.

50 The most common catchphrase is "The Bob Dylan of Brazil": http://www.nytimes.com/1992/09/09/garden/

lunch-with-caetano-veloso-lots-rebellion-little-hot-sauce-
for-spirited-bob-dylan.html?pagewanted=all (accessed
19 March 2017).

51 http://www.nytimes.com/2015/12/12/arts/music/
memorable-sinatra-moments.html/ It's interesting as well
to consider Iggy Pop's recollection of Sinatra's televized
encounter with Elvis Presley, in which "Frank showed
incredible pluck and guts in holding his own gracefully"
beside The King. I talk about it below.

52 http://www.villagevoice.com/music/we-got-a-lot-6407613
(accessed 19 March 2017).

53 Having invoked the notion of postmodern meta-narrative,
perhaps this is the moment to note one particularity
about the analyses of individual tracks that I'll put forth
in the following chapters: I've reordered them. In recent
years, the digitization of music, user-made playlists and
"shuffle" mode have diminished our sense of the linear
structure of albums, but to me track order is still immensely
significant. Sometimes it appears to indicate the flow of
mood and tempo that an artist intends, and sometimes
it can even mount an implicit narrative. I think there's a
possible reading of both of these logics in relation to the
track order on *A Foreign Sound*, but there's also a strong
possibility that the seeming *disorder* of the tracks is part of
the meta-commentary on how the world makes sense of
an overwhelming body of stylistically and historically diffuse
music from the U.S. The strongest argument for that reading,
in fact, is the liner notes, in which the tracks are listed
completely out of order—without any rationale whatsoever.
My own analyses will appear to have a kind of orderly logic

(vaguely chronological, and generic, occasionally conjoining two songs in a single section in order to highlight the connections between them)—but the relations I make between the songs will be, like my readings of them, personal and associative.

54 "The greatest act of vengeance used by the savages, and the one that seems to them most cruel and debasing, is to eat their enemy."

55 From my place, you also heard sometimes a young French woman who'd come to Brazil to learn to play guitar. She and her bossa nova teacher, who was also her lover, would practice into the night. My neighbor Gê, who'd rented me my tiny place, also loved music, and one evening he invited me over for a little impromptu performance by his friend, Jorge Mautner, who's also an old friend of Caetano's. They'd spent time together in London back in the day, and they'd go on to record an album together in 2002. I told the story of that miniature concert in *Samba*: "Jorge Mautner is an oddball of a Brazilian, from his incongruous name to his bluegrass fiddle playing and his fanatic tai chi training … He is the composer of the great socialist anthem, 'The Color of My Party's Flag Is Red.' But the night he came up to my hill, he said, 'Let's remember some of those sophisticated old sambas …'" (162). There was something profoundly melancholy to me that night about both the nostalgia of those old sambas, and also the seemingly perpetually deferred utopian politics of Mautner's most famous song, which he didn't sing. His friend Caetano has always had a more ambivalent relationship to left-wing politics in Brazil, and certainly to the Communist Party, though his most recent album includes a song ("Um Comunista") with a line that I'm sure spoke both to and for Mautner, as it does for me, and for many: "Vida sem utopia, *não entendo que exista.*" *Life without utopia, I cannot conceive of as existing.*

56 Veloso, Tropical Truth, op cit. 156.

57 Claude Lévi-Strauss, *Tristes Tropiques*, tr. John and Doreen Weightman (New York: Washington Square Press, 1977), 75.

Standards

The Carioca

Olha que coisa mais linda, mais cheia de graça,
É ela, menina que vem e que passa …[1]
VINÍCIUS DE MORAES AND ANTONIO CARLOS JOBIM,
"A GAROTA DE IPANEMA"

Say, have you seen the Carioca?
It's not a foxtrot or a polka …
GUS KAHN, EDWARD ELISCU AND VINCENT YOUMANS,
"THE CARIOCA"

A Foreign Sound opens with "The Carioca," ostensibly, that is, in Guanabara Bay—in Rio de Janeiro, in Brazil—which is to say, in Caetano's backyard. As I noted above, if he'd chosen to, he probably could have gotten away with including the emblematic paean to Rio, "The Girl from Ipanema," on his American Songbook album—in fact, maybe it simply would have been *too* obvious to begin with the song that radically torqued the notion of '60s jazz standards in the direction of Brazil.

Perhaps you're familiar with the story—you're certainly familiar with the tune. On the occasion of "The Girl from Ipanema"'s fiftieth anniversary, *The Wall Street Journal* ran a story by Thomas Vinciguerra that began, with an alarming lack of self-consciousness: "Before 1962, if John Q. Nobody gave any thought to South America at all, it probably didn't range much beyond banana republics, fugitive Nazis and Carmen Miranda." Vinciguerra goes on to say that all that "changed 50 years ago this summer when a tall and tan and young and lovely goddess was born."[2] While some U.S. listeners had already encountered bossa nova through earlier recordings by Stan Getz and Charlie Byrd, it was Getz's collaborative album with João Gilberto—*Getz/Gilberto*, which was actually released in 1964—that doused the world in the "seductive tropical cocktail" of bossa. The first track on that album was "The Girl from Ipanema," which opens with João singing Vinícius de Moraes's original Portuguese lyric, before introducing his then-wife Astrud Gilberto's restrained rendering of Norman Gimbel's English translation. Vinciguerra says, "While Mr. Gilberto's soft Portuguese sets the tone for the song, it is his wife's English response that still captivates after all this time. By all rights, it shouldn't." His accounting of Astrud Gilberto's inadequacies includes not only her musical inexperience,[3] but also her mangling of the pronunciation and—worse—the grammar of Gimbel's lyric. Apparently accommodating for the shift from a lovelorn male narrator to a more removed female observer, Astrud opted not to sing, "She looks straight ahead, not at me," but rather, "not at he." Vinciguerra says that Gimbel was "tearing [his] hair out" over that one—but argues that "when combined with her tentative delivery, Mr. Getz's breathy sax and Mr. Jobim's gentle piano, the errors make the result ever so slightly foreign—just out of reach, like the girl herself, and thus irresistible."

A foreign sound.

Though composed and first popularized by Brazilians, "The Girl from Ipanema" was quickly subsumed as a jazz standard—and ultimately it came to signify, for many listeners, the epitome of "easy listening" or "elevator music"— that unobtrusive ambient genre intended to herd us, docile, through the economic and architectural structures of mass consumption. It was a particularly cruel (or at least ironic) fate for a song and a style that, in fact, was arguably asking people to listen with a great deal of focus and attention. Caetano's most recent album, *Abraçaço*, includes a song called "A bossa nova é foda," which might be best rendered in English "Bossa Nova is the Fucking Shit." The earthiness of the title—and the song's arrangement and delivery, toggling between gravel-voiced, driving rock and the cool understatement of bossa itself—underscores the argument of the lyric: João Gilberto is hailed as the "wizard of Juazeiro" (the Bahian town of his birth) who supplied his poet-master with the musical artillery to slaughter any degraded or degrading images of the nation—and here the lyric segues into a list of famously lethal Brazilian boxers and mixed martial artists. The catalogue of Brazilian personifications of brute force is, of course, intended as a cocksure overturning of our collective failure to hear the challenge that João Gilberto and Tom Jobim represented. And it doesn't even matter, we're told, "if the romantic Jewish bard of Minnesota, the swineherd Eumaeus" recognizes or not that it's his master Odysseus returning to Ithaca—after bossa was born, nothing could ever be the same. It doesn't matter if Dylan could see or not João's greatness. It's a grand claim, but one that's both moving and compelling in its hyperbole.

And in fact, as Caetano pointed out to me,[4] Dylan actually *was* attuned to the radical challenges that bossa nova posed to listeners. But the movement's revolutionary nature hasn't been readily apprehended by many U.S. listeners. And maybe that explains, at least in part, why Caetano would choose not to hand over to the American Songbook a song, and a musical idiom, that's been heard here, so often, in a way that so badly misconstrues it.

So though he might have begun his exploration of *A Foreign Sound* in the misapprehended Rio of "The Girl from Ipanema," uncannily transformed in the echo chamber of that song's "American" standardization, Caetano chose instead to begin in an even weirder place, suspended somewhere mid-air between the U.S. and Brazil—a completely imaginary "Latin" paradise conjured for the 1933 cinematic fantasy, *Flying Down to Rio*. The film was the first on-screen partnering of Fred Astaire and Ginger Rogers, who are depicted observing, and then performing, a novelty dance named after the residents of the city that supposedly spawned it: "The Carioca." Since this was their first appearance together, RKO Pictures started billing Astaire and Rogers as "The King and Queen of 'The Carioca'"—though the dance turned out not to have legs: it never took off as a popular social dance form.[5]

Carioca is a word of Tupi origin that's used as both an adjective and a substantive in reference to anything or anyone from Rio. Which the "Carioca" of *Flying Down to Rio* most certainly isn't. In the film, the song is performed by Etta Moten Barnett, Movita Castañeda, and Alice Gentle,[6] and its choreography is a peculiar literalization of the bridge:

evoking the truism that "two heads are better than one," the lyric instructs the dancers to join forces. Lest you think this might be a reference to the possibilities of intercultural (as in Getz/Gilberto) or even interpersonal (as in Fred and Ginger, or João and Astrud) collaboration, the choreography makes it clear: it's just about a dance whose defining characteristic is that the partners maintain their foreheads pressed together. As Ginger bemusedly asks Fred, "What's the deal with the foreheads?" The detail is used to comic effect when Fred and Ginger one-up the ostensibly Brazilian dancers at their own dance, with a momentary glitch when they accidentally bonk each other's noggin. That is, the "Carioca" seems potentially erotically charged, but also somewhat goofy and a little dangerous.

That "clop" of foreheads banging together is percussively replicated in the thwack of a *timbau* that begins Caetano's arrangement: "brack brrrrroom, brack brack, boom boom, brack brack brack, boom boom." Laced among the beats are the syncopated accents of an electric guitar, and, as the song progresses, increasing, spare layers of more percussion, drums, and bass, all highly panned, adding to the sense of cock-eyed, unpredictable and yet somehow restrained playfulness. As I mentioned, many of the arrangements on *A Foreign Sound* bear a resemblance to Nelson Riddle's elegant chamber orchestrations on Sinatra's *Close to You*—though sometimes with a certain "saltiness," in Christgau's words. The arrangement of "The Carioca," though, foregrounds percussion—particularly contemporary Bahian percussion, sounded by the *timbau*[7]— and the spare harmonic instrumentation is electric. Caetano's version of "The Carioca," then, is clearly updated—and is animated by the very sounds that animate current "authentic" Brazilian popular music. If I place "authentic" in scare quotes, it's not to ironize that sound. But it's to say that, while "The Carioca" of 1933 was clearly an imaginary Brazilian music and dance form, Caetano's ensconcing of the song in the sounds of contemporary Brazil only highlights the disjunction of any effort to isolate Brazilian or U.S. sounds—or, for that matter, African and Iberian sounds.

And of course winding through all that is that voice: mercurial, with its undecidable hint of irony.

I'll Take Manhattan

I'll take Manhattan, the Bronx, and Staten Island too …
LORENZ HART (WITH RICHARD RODGERS), "MANHATTAN"

Deusa da lenda na proa
Levanta uma torcha na maõ …[8]
CAETANO VELOSO, "MANHATÃ"

Yesterday I walked to the edge of the Hudson and looked downstream across the glinting surface of the water toward the Statue of Liberty. There she was, seeming to be looking back upstream at me, over her shoulder, lifting her torch in a quiet and subtle gesture of personal communion. Not an ironic gesture, but one tinged with faint melancholy.[9] What does it mean that the face of my own city and nation are most recognizable to me—and most beautiful to me—in the lyric of a song that Caetano wrote with a refrain that intentionally twists the pronunciation of this island into a Brazilian sound? *Manhatã* …

Caetano has said that this is one of his favorite compositions, holding "true echoes of my sentiment for New York." The song is dedicated to the Brazilian pop star Lulu Santos, who once uttered the intentionally estranging/familiarizing pronunciation of the island's name to Caetano, who was reminded of a similar gesture by the *concretistas* in a citation of the poet Sousândrade.[10] "Manhatã" was recorded on Caetano's 1998 *Livro*, and in the liner notes he says that a "re-listening" to recordings of cool jazz led him to ask Jaques Morelenbaum for an arrangement that would mix "modern Bahian street percussion [the very rhythms they would later inject into "The Carioca"] with sophisticated cool sounds."[11] The strangely perfect combination of Brazilian and U.S. musical vocabularies is redoubled in "Manhatã" by the sounding of language— a point Caetano made explicit in a mini-lecture when he performed the song live in a joint concert with David Byrne in New York. Here is Ben Ratliff's retelling of that event in the New York Times:

> And then there was "Manhata," [*sic*] whose aerated brass arrangements bring to mind the Miles Davis–Gil Evans collaborations of the late 50's; it's a song about Manhattan inspired by the writing of a 19th-century Brazilian poet [Sousândrade]. "As we learned the name from the English colonizers, we accept Manhattan as an English word," Mr. Veloso explained, entering his professorial mode. "But if we say it this way,

it sounds like a Brazilian Indian word, and that creates a subversive Pan-Americanism."[12]

Maybe the explication of the complexity of pronunciation came across as professorial from the concert stage, but in the lyric of the song itself it's extremely affecting—as is the feminization of the metropolis in an indigenous American girl's name. The feminization of metropolitan or—particularly—national symbols isn't always so poignant—and doesn't always preclude the invocation of those symbols to brutal ends. The same could be said of indigeneity. But when a Brazilian tongue rubs up against the colonial tongue that rubbed up against an indigenous American language construed as feminine, and extended as Pan-American, what happens is simultaneously subversive and very tender.

But "Manhatã" is rubbing up against something else, which is not only the pronunciation of "Manhattan," but also its place in the history of song. Because you can't write a song about Manhattan without invoking "Manhattan"—a track located at the very heart of *A Foreign Sound*. For all its iconic stature, Rodgers and Hart's song—both in its jaunty, tripping melody and its comical lyric—seems resolutely self-abnegating. In fact, its iconicity seems to *rest* on its comic humility. That's surely one of the ironies of U.S. popular song—its global prominence is founded in part on its insistence that it's low-brow. Self-abnegation is also the quality played up by many of the best known interpretations of this particular song. Allan Gould, who sang it in 1929 with Ruth Lester, pulls a self-mocking pseudo-British accent on the words "fahhhncy" and

"Delahhhncey". Mel Tormé hams up the British "fahhhncy" only to go all-out Lower East Side on "Delyaaancey," highlighting the joke.[13] The basic story of the song—clearer if one includes the opening strophe, which Caetano skips, about not having the cash for a trip to "Niag'ra"[14]—is that a young couple will make the best of having to stay in the city for the summer. I remember my mother explaining to me—I must have been about ten at the time, and I'd never been to New York—that the song's claims about the romantic scents and sounds of the borough in mid-July were tongue-in-cheek. (Now that I've lived here for most of my life, I'm still vaguely befuddled when people complain about the way the city smells in the summer: It smells like New York! It's romantic!) In 1925, when the song was written, the streets and sights conjured by the lyric were working-class, to say the least—and ethnically demarcated. Tormé's inflection on "Delyaaancey" is mild compared with Hart's overt inscription of an accent that one can call "New York," but has definite class and ethnic implications when it invokes "the dreams of a boy and goil."

So what happens when Caetano takes in that mouthful of cultural specificity? The funny thing about that line is, it's the one place in the song where he sounds most "foreign"— but not on "goil." It's the city's "clamor" that rings strange, the "a" long, not short. There's nothing forced in his diction in his singing of the song—it's neither fake-formal nor jokey low-brow. He seems to take pleasure in Hart's punny proliferation of internal rhymes, and all that alliteration (So many fricatives! So many glottal stops!). So what happens when part of the charm of that poetry has so much to do with something so very specific, not just to "American" language, or even to the metropolis of New York, but to the Yiddish-inflected Lower East Side? In precisely the place where you'd think the specificity of the lyric might estrange him the most, he makes his own modification—but maybe not the one you'd expect: in the final strophe, he changes the dreams of a girl and boy to those of "a Jew and goy." I looked everywhere to see who else did this. I was sure Blossom Dearie must have, somewhere—it seemed like if anybody could be that coyly funny it would be her. But she didn't. A commenter on a blog about Yiddish said that he and "everybody he knew" made that change when they sang the song, but the only recording he could cite was Caetano's.[15] It's a joke you'd think Hart would have made. He came so close to making it himself! It doesn't sound like a joke Caetano would make. But then again—why not?[16]

Richard Rodgers and Lorenz Hart were Jewish—as were Oscar Hammerstein, Irving Berlin, Jerome Kern, the Gershwin Brothers, and Leonard Bernstein. The predominance of Jewish composers in the American Songbook isn't news, though it continues to feel revelatory for many casual listeners who haven't given much thought to the cultural provenance of *Oklahoma!*, *Porgy and Bess* or *West Side Story*. In fact, a recent PBS documentary on the Jewish composition of the American Songbook went so far as to make an oblique claim on the one obvious outlier, "Episcopalian Cole Porter, [who]… after three Broadway flops, finally ascertained the surefire way to success: 'I'm going to write Jewish tunes.'"[17] It's no secret—and yet the very openness of the enigma seems to make it disappear: many of the songs that are held, within the Songbook, to give voice to (to use the language of the time of their composition) "all-American" (white, Christian), as well as "Negro" and "Hispanic" identity, were written by composers steeped in the music of the Jewish diaspora. But when the complexity of "American" cultural identity in popular song is voiced by a Brazilian singer, for whom the ironies resonate in a very specific way, "Manhattan" begins to have a very strange sound—but it's not the strangeness of Caetano's foreignness. It's the strangeness of our own incapacity to hear the dissonances in our notions of U.S. cultural and ethnic identity. For all that, the arrangement of "Manhattan" on *A Foreign Sound* is very simple:[18] Caetano's lilting voice is counterbalanced only by Jaques Morelenbaum's equally relaxed and graceful cello. Caetano's vocal line is droll rather than comical, gently gliding, for instance, over the pushcarts that are themselves "gently gli-i-iding by." His "*t*"s have a clipped specificity that's not superior—just elegant. Morelenbaum alternates his own nimble little maneuvers around the melody with a few brusque double-stops and strummed pizzicato chords.

The duet has a grace that's reminiscent, for me, of another partnering around the song, one half of which I've already invoked. Aside from Caetano's, Blossom Dearie's[19] is the version I've listened to the most (though, as you will have noticed, repeated listenings didn't prevent me from misremembering her version of the lyric). I'm not actually referring to her partnering with Ray Brown or Jo Jones, who accompany Dearie on bass and drums with their customary sophistication, taste and discretion. I'm referring to Bill T. Jones's choreographic interpretation of Dearie's version that was a brief moment of utter perfection in his 1990 *Breathing Show*. What Bill T. Jones managed to pull out of Dearie's quietly mischievous take on the song was its very slight, romantic obscenity, a little bit of naughtiness—a faint whiff, as it were, of Mott Street in July—none of which diminished the sincere love of the city (or the song) at its core. These two duets—of a Brazilian Jew and goy, and of a subtle, girlish blonde jazz pianist and a sublimely graceful, queer-identified black choreographer—both seem to me, from what might appear to be their skewed angles on a love song about a New York "girl and boy," to find the heart of the song. The place it becomes strange—and to me, most beautiful.

Always / So in Love

I'll be loving you, always
With a love that's true, always.
IRVING BERLIN, "ALWAYS"

Eu sei que vou te amar
Por toda a minha vida eu vou te amar …[20]
ANTONIO CARLOS JOBIM AND VINÍCIUS DE MORAES, "EU SEI QUE VOU TE AMAR"

Strange dear, but true dear.
COLE PORTER, "SO IN LOVE"

Apenas te peço que aceite
O meu estranho amor.[21]
CAETANO VELOSO, "NOSSO ESTRANHO AMOR"

George S. Kaufman once said that, when he heard the song "Always," he tried to convince his friend Irving Berlin to be a little more realistic and change it to, "I'll be Loving You Thursday." But Berlin was an "incurable romantic" (Kaufman said he himself was "curable"). The title—and the refrain—stuck.[22] While a song like "Manhattan" exemplifies the American Songbook's apparently self-abnegating sense of humor and irony, "Always" demonstrates that there's still room for unabashed—and unironic—romanticism. Berlin wrote "Always" in 1925 as a wedding gift for his second wife, Ellin McKay (his first wife, Dorothy Goetz, died at the age of twenty of typhoid fever, which she contracted during their honeymoon). Berlin's relationship with McKay was, by all accounts, harmonious to the end, so evidently his "incurable" romanticism—and optimism—weren't misplaced.

Unrestrained and unabashed romance is certainly also a part of the tradition of Brazilian songwriting, and the most celebrated composers of popular song gave themselves over to both musical and lyrical expressions of it. Though his domestic history was more varied and populous than Berlin's (he'd racked up eight marriages before his death at sixty-six in 1980), Vinícius de Moraes was also an incurable romantic, and "Eu sei que vou te amar" is merely one of a number of lyrics that derive their emotional force from the extremity of the protestation of love, combined with Jobim's opulent musicality. The song's been covered by a wide range of Brazilian artists, including João Gilberto and Caetano himself.[23] That is to say, Caetano has explored the terrain of lush romanticism in the Brazilian Songbook as well. His own catalogue of love songs includes works of extraordinary tenderness, but the most moving of them lean toward either understatement or internal struggle, as opposed to the gushing avowals of either "Always" or "Eu sei que vou te amar."

The only English-language book-length consideration of his oeuvre, Lorraine Leu's *Brazilian Popular Music: Caetano Veloso and the Regeneration of Tradition*, dedicates one chapter to "The Tradition of Love Song in Brazil"[24] and another to "Unidentifiable Objects of Desire: Caetano Veloso's Love Songs."[25] Leu concludes her historical overview of the genre by arguing that Caetano's take on it since his early grappling with the military dictatorship has actually been a politically charged exploration of the "interaction between imagination and reality." Which may explain why, in her chapter on Caetano's "love songs," she focusses on a number of compositions that most listeners would group under a very different rubric— largely songs of social critique, in which an oblique moment of address to a lover gives narrative context to the political rumination.[26]

There are songs in Caetano's discography—both covers and originals—that fit much more obviously into the category of "love songs." In fact, on *Uns* (1983), yet another unapologetically romantic lyric by Vinícius de Moraes ("Coisa mais linda,"—"Most Beautiful Thing"—with music by Carlos Lyra) is followed immediately by Caetano's own "Você é linda,"—"You are Beautiful"—a seeming answer in kind. I'll go on to say more about "Você é linda" in my consideration of Caetano's take on pop, but suffice it to say here that he isn't averse to absolutist romantic declarations: "*Você é linda, mais que demais.*

Você é linda, sim …" (You are beautiful, more than too much. You are beautiful, yes …) There are other stranger, more carnal lines in the song, evoking muscle, tooth, and bone—it's not a simplistic or predictable lyric—but the refrain is as definitive in its romantic exaltation as Berlin's.

Fourteen years after "Você é linda," Caetano would compose "Você é minha" ("You are Mine," on *Livro*)—with clear echoes of his own prior composition. He wrote in the liner notes of the latter song that he and his frequent arranger Morelenbaum "reinforced the similarities to *'Você é linda'* because we thought it was funny, the illusion that I have my own style of love song."[27] If he *does* have his own style of love song, the defining characteristic would surely not be the extremity of his declarations of love, but rather the moments that are, well, a little strange. Or very strange. Moments of unusual quietude. Or, on the contrary, moments with teeth, muscles—even mucous. Even bile.

Among the love songs of extreme understatement, to my ear the most delicately affecting is "Minha mulher" ("My Wife," on *Jóia*, 1975).[28] From the outside, Caetano sings, one might think his wife was the childlike one, like a daughter—but in fact, she's like a mother. He repeats this. And then sings, simply, *"Meu bichinho bonito, meu bichinho bonito, meu bichinho bonito …"* (My beautiful little critter …) *"Minha mulher, minha mulher, minha mulher …"* The guitar is a guileless progression of repeating minor and major seventh chords, looping, looping. The voice is like a kitten's mew.

But he's also capable of expressing love as an angry howl. On *Cê*, the first of his recent trilogy of chamber rock albums with the "Banda Cê,"[29] Caetano recorded a song that might seem to be an even more attenuated example of a "love song" than those categorized as such by Leu: "Odeio" ("I Hate"). At the apparent terminus of a relationship, the narrator finds himself adrift. He recounts the dream-like possibilities that opened before him: a stream of ready and willing lovers, mucose, slippery with desire, a radiant girl smiling like a dolphin, a beautiful, angelic young man, each one saying "yes ..." But the singer derides himself as aging, ugly, negligible. And then comes the stunning refrain: "*Odeio você. Odeio você. Odeio você. Odeio.*" (I hate you. I hate you. I hate you. I hate.) It's perhaps the most extreme, touching, and vulnerable expression of love, and utter loss.

In her consideration of Caetano's apprehension of the significance of the love song, perhaps Leu's most compelling— and convincing—suggestion is that his "Não identificado" ("Unidentified," on the 1969 White Album) might be retitled: "How to Write a Love Song."[30] Indeed, the song begins, "*Eu vou fazer uma canção pra ela, uma canção singela, brasileira* ..." (I'm going to make a song for her, a simple, Brazilian song ...) The singer says he'll strategically release it right after the carnival, but the song should be recorded on a flying saucer, released into outer space ... He says his passion should shine in the night sky of a small town in the Brazilian backlands like a UFO ... Romantic love, that is, should be the occasion for making songs that can simultaneously speak to the heart of a nation, and seem completely alien.

In listening to the convergence of "Ipanema," "The Carioca," "Manhatã" and "Manhattan," I suggested that one's love of one's city or country can become more poignant when that attachment is somehow made strange. Of course, the same can be said of one's love of one's lover. "Strange dear, but true dear." Cole Porter's "So in Love" was originally written in 1948 for the musical *Kiss Me Kate*, which was adapted into a film by George Sidney in 1953. As I've already mentioned, this musical, and this song in particular, are often cited as evidence of Porter's purported desire to "write Jewish songs." In the post-war period, Porter's minor-key ballad may have contributed, ironically, to an Eastern European slant in the American Songbook. But it's been skewed in other directions as well. In 1990, k.d. lang recorded a cover of it for the AIDS benefit album, *Red Hot + Blue*. She also appeared in an extraordinary music video directed by Percy Adlon. *Red Hot + Blue*, comprised entirely of Cole Porter covers, was the first in a series of albums benefiting PWAs,[31] and its release also occasioned a series of music videos—among them lang and Adlon's.

It wasn't coincidental that the Red Hot + Blue organization chose the music of Cole Porter for its first benefit album. At the height of the AIDS pandemic, it was a knowing and dignified move to draw the world's attention to the fact that one of the central figures in the American Songbook had lived, relatively openly for the period, as a gay man. Many of the other Porter covers on *Red Hot + Blue* make the old standards sound unfamiliar—often by infusing them with the rhythms and instrumentation of hip-hop, neo-soul, alternative rock, or techno. lang's version of "So in Love" is slightly tango-inflected, with a smoky accordion line running through it, but the arrangement is by no means a stretch for a mid-century standard. Neither is lang's vocal interpretation, which Lori Burns has characterized as a "great tribute to the original song and its composer," even as the corresponding video's images could be understood as "appropriating and recontextualizing the genre of the 'torch song.'"[32] The recontextualizing Burns indicates here is the implicit narrative in the video, which shows lang looking characteristically handsome, in mannish attire, but tending to domestic labor typically understood as "women's work." She's doing laundry and straightening up a domestic space. But as the video progresses, the details (the boiling of some feminine garments on a stove, apparently to disinfect them, the presence of some medical equipment, including an IV bag of amber fluid) construct a narrative: she's cleaning up after a dead or possibly dying same-sex lover. She buries her face in her lover's filmy white nightgown as her mezzo-soprano voice recalls her initial delirium at "the thought that you might care." There are of course various unexpected inversions—the musical standard queered (or shown in its always-already queerness), the heartache transferred from a narrative of "the battle between the sexes" to one of a devastating illness, and finally the flipping of the notion of AIDS as an exclusively male disease, while gesturing toward its impact on same-sex couples.

In the stage version of *Kiss Me Kate*, "So in Love" is performed by the estranged but still amorous ex-wife Lilli in the first act. In the last act, it's reprised by her ex-husband, Fred, with whom she's destined to reunite. That is, it does its own flip, not only on gender, but also on the Shakespearean drama[33] that is the story within the story of the musical. There are notable recorded versions by both men and women. There's nothing unusual about either a mezzo-soprano or a baritenor taking on the song. The estrangement, and the ache of it, in the song crosses gender. It has to do with the inherent strangeness in love itself, perhaps most bruised and sensitive in the divided couple (think: "Odeio").

Caetano's version of "So in Love" is among the lushest of the orchestral arrangements on *A Foreign Sound*, opening with the plaintive wail of violins, soon joined by the deeper moans of the rest of a string ensemble, and finally Lula Galvão's understated acoustic guitar (merely marking, in large part, the upbeats) and Marcelo Costa's tempered second-beat cymbal accents. Caetano's voice enters in that baritone range I spoke of, the one it's hard to hear as such: "Strange dear, but true dear." The word "strange," in fact, is strange—precisely that deepest of notes that doesn't immediately reveal its depth. Even stranger is the "even" of the second stanza ("Even without you, my arms fold about you"). It's the long, slightly aspirated "*eeeehven*" that has an uncanny, deep-throated quality. It's something he's long done in his low range—that aspirated *eeeh*. One of the most uncanny instances is on yet another of his own compositions that appears at the very end of his 1978 album *Muito*—a song that appears to announce itself most explicitly as a "love song" in its title: "Eu te amo." I love you. But despite the seeming insistence of its lyric ("I love you, I'm going to say I love you, yes …"), and despite the ultra-romantic piano-and-voice arrangement of the song, obviously evoking Jobim, there are two elements that make it a peculiar, and somewhat distancing, performance of "love." One is that weird, aspirated *eeeh* on the word *azeviche*[34]—so low and breathy one could almost call his technique here extended. And the other is the very last line of the lyric: "*Serei pra sempre o teu cantor.*" (I'll always be your singer.) Yours, singular. Your singular singer. Which means that, as a love song, it's directed to every listener, who longs to hear it as a singular address—but has to confront the impossibility of the singularity of the address, since it's going out to every listener of this "radio voice" that seeps out everywhere, and attaches to none.

There's one other composition of his that appears to espouse an almost Buddhist non-attachment in love, even as it embraces "crazy desire": "Nosso estranho amor" (Our Strange Love).[35] The singer doesn't want to use up his lover, to lay waste to her, or to claim her as a mere ornament. He just wants her to respect his own mad desire. He doesn't care if she has other lovers, as long as they give her pleasure. "*Apenas te peço que aceite o meu estranho amor.*" (I just want you to accept my strange love.) It's another kind of distancing that is, in its distancing, strangely cherishing, and in its claim to multiplicity, singularly devoted.

The Man I Love / Love for Sale

He'll look at me and smile.
I'll understand.
GEORGE AND IRA GERSHWIN, "THE MAN I LOVE"

Who's prepared to pay the price,
For a trip to paradise?
COLE PORTER, "LOVE FOR SALE"

As I said, "So in Love" is a song that was written to be sung across genders. But there are two standards on *A Foreign Sound* that are anything but obvious choices for a male singer: another Porter tune, "Love for Sale," and the Gershwin brothers' "The Man I Love." Actually, Tony Bennett recorded the former in 1976, as did Mel Tormé in 1988, and Harry Connick in 1999, but Bennett and Tormé altered the lyrics to suggest a female protagonist in the third person. Connick didn't—and neither did Caetano. The implications of Bennett and Tormé's third-person narration of the story of a world-weary streetwalker, or of Connick's voicing of that story in the first person, are perhaps suspended.[36] I'll try to unpack some of the possible implications of Caetano's own version in a moment. But in regard to an overt overturning of gender expectations, the even more marked track is "The Man I Love."

It's certainly not the first time Caetano's subverted gender expectations in song.[37] His 1979 *Cinema Transcendental* includes his much-loved composition "Menino do Rio" ("The Boy from Rio"). He wrote it for the female pop singer Baby Consuelo to sing in the soundtrack of a telenovela in

1980—but he didn't hesitate to record his own version. The title clearly references "The Girl from Ipanema," but this time the perfect, tanned beach creature has a dragon tattoo on his arm. It's a song of utter enchantment. The narrator leans back to observe the carefree splendor of muscular youth, and sings, like a sigh, "*Toma esta canção como um beijo …*" (Take this song like a kiss.) When Caetano sings it, it's gorgeously homoerotic, and utterly pure. It's been recorded by a range of Brazilian artists, mostly women, but men as well, and it would be extremely reductive to suggest that the versions by men are intended as explicit statements regarding sexuality. Some, maybe. Mostly not. In *Tropical Truth*, Caetano briefly marvels that João Gilberto recorded a version. He changed nary a word.

Caetano's been pressed any number of times to directly address his own sexual identity. He explicitly takes up the question toward the end of his memoir, in a chapter describing his return to Brazil after his period in exile. That was, of course, a period in which British rock stars were intentionally provoking questions about gender and sexuality through both personal style and ambiguous public statements. Caetano was also interested in provocation—but not just in the sphere of sexuality. "When I returned from London in 1972, the subtle imitation of Carmen Miranda I'd woven into my performance of '*O que é que a baiana tem?*' amounted to a double commentary: it spoke to the meaning of Brazilian pop art in exile, and to the originality of the potential Brazilian contribution to the cause of sexual liberation."[38] I've already written of the complexity and nuance in his apprehension of

Carmen's pop dimension. His take on "the potential Brazilian contribution to the cause of sexual liberation" is equally complex, and in fact intricately related to that other question.

When he raises the issue in his book—nearly at the end of it—Caetano writes: "It is necessary to speak about sex here. But what should be said first is that there is nothing more difficult to speak about."[39] He expresses his distaste for the contemporary voyeuristic/exhibitionistic cult of sexual intrigue in the mass media, even as he rejects nostalgia for an age of secrecy and taboo. He says that sex has remained for him since childhood both thoroughly natural and profoundly mystical. He recounts a Rorschach test he underwent at the age of twenty-three, which indicated "'latent homosexuality; female identification; idealization of women.'"[40] This, despite the intensely satisfying erotic relationship he was enjoying with his (future) wife. Still, he didn't reject the suggestions out of hand. The Rorschach test also indicated a talent for music. This he found more surprising. He always thought he'd make a much better filmmaker than singer, his more obvious gifts being visual and verbal. He says he also thinks he'd probably make a great queer. But his sexual history—including the long, committed domestic relationships he maintained sequentially with his two wives—stands. On his successes as both a musician and a sexual partner of women, he declares: "I consider myself more successful than I deserve to be."[41]

It's a characteristically complex summation: neither an outright espousal of a hard-and-fast sexual identity, nor a capitulation to a vague, convenient in-between status of "bisexuality"—a term that irks him.[42] It's also characteristic in its simultaneous modesty and implicit hubris. "The sexual indeterminacy that had intrigued boys in school and which I incorporated into my public persona from the sixties onward bespeaks profound notions concerning the nature of my desires as well as my choice of roles."[43] If he's chosen roles, they're not always indeterminate. His 2006 song, "Homem" ("Man"), is emphatic: he doesn't envy maternity, lactation, adiposity, or menstruation. The only things he envies women are their greater life expectancy and multiple orgasms. "*Eu sou homem, pêlo grosso no nariz.*" (I'm man, thick hair in my nose.)

His version of "The Man I Love" is no caricature—of masculinity, of effeminacy, or indeterminacy. It has—here I hesitated and couldn't come up with anything more accurate than his own description of Sinatra's "sober, dignified manliness" on *Close to You*. Which in no way precludes that openness to homoeroticism or to a feminine perspective that the Rorschach foretold. The track is another of those Nelson Riddle-style arrangements, again overlaying the winds and strings (and Morelenbaum's gracious cello solo) with spare, syncopated acoustic guitar and pulled-back percussion. The vocal, too, is pulled back (the final four words, "the man I love," are particularly understated—almost shy). And it's sincerely romantic, perhaps in the way that only a song can be that's about a completely hypothetical love.[44]

There is, in fact, one other male cover of the song that I should mention—though to call it a cover is perhaps a stretch. It's a version I've written about before, one I love very much: Lutz Förster performing the song in American Sign Language over the 1928 recording of Sophie Tucker singing it. This dance (it is a dance, as much as it is a silent voicing of the song) was incorporated into Pina Bausch's 1982 choreography, *Carnations*, and it appears in Chantal Akerman's 1983 documentary film, *Un jour Pina m'a demandé* ... In a novel I wrote, my narrator describes Förster as he appears in that film: "You can faintly hear him moaning ... His hands are so beautiful. The sign for *maybe* is a kind of indecisive wobbling of both hands, palms up ... When Tucker sings 'just built for two,' Förster holds up two long, thin fingers in the shape of a *V*. He signs *roam* by tracing a zig-zagging line before him. 'Who would, would you?' ends with a wavering gesture, half pointing out, half pulling back ..." Reflecting on that equivocal dance, the narrator says, "'Some day he'll come along, the man I love.' Some day. But right now, Lutz Förster is wobbling his empty hands, zig-zagging an aimless trail, wavering his extended thumb and his pinky finger before him in some vague question in the conditional. 'Who would, would you?'"[45]

What moved my narrator in Lutz Förster's interpretation of Sophie Tucker's interpretation of the song is very close to what moves me in Caetano's version. In fact, Caetano's tender enunciation of "just built for two," with the *two* so subtly aspirated, is precisely evocative of the delicacy of Förster's long, thin fingers in the shape of a *V*. It would be radically simplifying things to say that that dance is a silent voicing of homosexual desire—or that the sung version is its enunciation. They both express much more and less than that: the love of a love that doesn't yet exist.[46]

But to move from idealized love to love down and dirty, and all too experiential: "Love for Sale" was written by Cole

Porter for the 1930 Broadway musical *The New Yorkers*, and in the first staged version it was sung by Kathryn Crawford, a white actress, with a trio of friends, in front of Reuben's Restaurant. But the public, it seems, wasn't quite ready to hear white womanhood besmirched in the jaded self-accounting of a sex worker. Critics and audiences balked. The song was banned from radio play. In January of 1931 the producers came up with a solution, short of cutting the song from the musical. They pulled Crawford out and replaced her with an African-American singer, Elisabeth Welch, and staged her singing about the "oldest profession" in front of the Cotton Club in Harlem. Evidently, this was a version of the story that audiences could take.

Despite the radio ban and the initial public resistance, "Love for Sale" eventually became a standard. It lay relatively fallow until jazz artists picked it up in the '40s and '50s. I've already said a bit about the notable recordings of it by men. Perhaps it's not surprising that the best-known women singers who have covered it are, in the majority, African-American, with the exception of everybody's favorite ethical slut, Julie London.[47] It's complicated to talk about the character of the song. Welch claimed an appreciation for the poetry of the lyrics,[48] and sang it with almost operatic brio. Billie Holiday recorded it with Oscar Peterson in 1952, and many consider her version to be definitive (I'll say more about that momentarily). Ella Fitzgerald sang it pretty much as if it were a romantic ballad—without much in the way of either pathos or a knowing wink. Eartha Kitt did it with lots of percussion, opening with whispered, breathy taunts. Dinah

Washington's version begins very slowly, almost mournfully, but suddenly, after a little growl, she picks up the mood, and the pace. Shirley Horn's version is smoky and gorgeous, long, deep, and hushed right up until the startlingly gutsy, almost defiant close. White singers, both women and men, have tended to emphasize the sardonic tone, or to make it a finger-snapping inside joke. London's version is vampy, and she practically chews on the words to get at their mordant potential. Diane Shuur's take is high show-biz. I already mentioned the interpretations of Bennett, Tormé, and Connick.

And Caetano's? It's nothing like that at all. It's perhaps the most dramatic track on *A Foreign Sound*, and one that many critics of the album singled out for its emotional force. I'm sure that has much to do with the fact that it's the only a cappella track on the album, but there are other possible reasons—perhaps it's his particular attentiveness to the language of the song. The poet and essayist Charles Bernstein cited Caetano's interpretation in his analysis of the lyric:

> One of the most recent covers of the song intensifies, more than any other I know, the foreignness at its heart; perhaps it is not surprising that the Brazilian musician and vocalist Caetano Veloso would—like Billie Holiday—bring out just how haunting and desolate "Love for Sale" is … Veloso knows just how to make the familiar strange.[49]

Bernstein makes this observation in the context of considering Cole Porter as a literary predecessor to other "difficult" (and gay) poets, Frank O'Hara and John Ashbery, both of whom, like Porter, incorporate references to ostensibly banal popular culture in their work. Bernstein calls Porter a kind of proto-pop artist in this respect—which of course resonates with Caetano's own preoccupation with pop art's aesthetic ramifications for popular song. But the peculiar thing about Bernstein's listening to Caetano's version of "Love for Sale" is not only that he hears echoes there of Porter's clever, subtle, and complex pop sensibility and "homotextuality," but that he also hears something of Billie Holiday.

Holiday's version is stupefying. Shirley Horn described Peterson's accompaniment like this: "Oscar spread flowers beneath her."[50] The vocal on the track is foregrounded—unusually so for a recording of Holiday—and you hear, more than ever, her breath, her lips, her swallowing, and the coy, highly personal spoken quality of the words. The "*p*"s—and there are a lot of them—are a little wet, and plosive. If other versions seem to choose between gloom and sarcasm, Holiday's remains in the eerie space between. Does she sound like she's been drinking? Sort of, in her apparent unselfconsciousness, but that's not the same as a lack of control. Her musicianship is extraordinary on the song. Still, there's a kind of self-relinquishing to the tawdry story—it's not self-mocking, but it's self-knowing, a near-whimper behind a half-smile. Of course, one wants to check one's romanticization of that performance. It's a bit too tempting to conflate Holiday's public persona, including her own storied past of adolescent conscription to sex work, with the dramatic narrative of the song. And still.

So why would Charles Bernstein find it "unsurprising" that Caetano, like Holiday, would be able to locate the troubling aspect of the song? Was hers the version that he studied in attempting to find his own? At moments, it certainly sounds like it. He doesn't take on any affectation that might explicitly reference her—there's none of that dipping, girlish conversational tone. But his "*p*"s are plosive and wet like hers, moist lips very close to your ear: "Who's prepared to pay the price for a trip to paradise?"[51] Why did he choose a barren ground, no petals strewn like those of Peterson under Holiday's fragile voice? Where Peterson strew petals, there's just aching silence—seemingly endless seconds of it.

Body and Soul

I'd gladly surrender myself to you, body and soul.
EDWARD HEYMAN, ROBERT SOUR, FRANK EYTON, AND JOHNNY GREEN, "BODY AND SOUL"

As souls unbodied, bodies unclothed must be …
JOHN DONNE, "ELEGY XIX (TO HIS MISTRESS GOING TO BED)"

"Body and Soul" was also banned from radio play in 1930, again because the self-narration of a carnal woman was considered excessive. But there's nothing in the lyric that explicitly marks it as a woman's lament, and there have been plenty of interpretations by both men and women, including

Holiday, Fitzgerald, Sinatra, Vaughan—and a striking duet by Tony Bennett and Amy Winehouse recorded shortly before Winehouse's death. There's also been a huge range of instrumental versions. Coleman Hawkins's wildly inventive 1939 tenor sax version is one of the most influential jazz recordings of all times. To my ear, the melodic and harmonic qualities of the song far surpass its somewhat awkward lyric, with its stilted grammatical inversions and clunky rhymes. Although maybe the stilt and clunk are part of the appeal. But the music is extraordinary, with its weird and arbitrary changes that still, somehow, manage to seem not just natural, but necessary. Musicians and critics rhapsodize over the bridge.[52]

Billie Holiday in fact recorded more than one version. Her 1957 studio album is titled after the track, and she's joined by a sextet, with solos by Ben Webster on tenor sax and Harry "Sweets" Edison on trumpet. But the intro belongs to Barney Kessel on electric guitar. It's a strange, arpeggiated chord—F Eb A Db Gb … I'm not even sure what that is. It hangs there for a second, completely disconcerting. Then there's a gentle strum of Bbm7, and Holiday's voice comes in—"My days have grown …"—with another disconcerting pause. So lonely.

She's the only one, I think, to sing the first line like that. Caetano's version begins like Ella's, Frank's, and Sarah's, just the way it was written: "My heart is sad and lonely." It's his own acoustic guitar that keeps the steady beat, with Ricardo Silveira's electric guitar lacing in and out. Silveira's tone evokes Kessel's, but his instrumental solo—with Zeca Assumpção bowing a subtle double bass behind—loops errantly around the melody with the kind of agility and evasiveness so many instrumentalists have demonstrated on the song since Hawkins first took his spin on it. Some vocalists have also looped around (Winehouse has a field day), and some sing it straight up. Caetano's vocal, like his guitar, is straightforward, with just a hint of João's slight rush-and-lag in his phrasing. There's also that granular quality, a little hoarseness, something physical. A hint of a smile. Something erotic.

What might the "surrender" of the song mean to him? Body and soul. The body, as I've said, appears in all its carnality in many of his songs: muscles, teeth, lips, hair, mucus, skin. Hilariously, one of the most carnal songs of all in his discography—"Elegia"—is a version of Augusto de Campos's translation of a section of John Donne's "Elegy XIX (To His Mistress Going to Bed)," with music by Péricles Cavalcanti.[53] It begins SHOCKINGLY: "*Deixa que minha mão errante adentre / atrás, na frente, em cima, em baixo …*" It's just as dirty in the original:

> Licence my roving hands, and let them go
> Before, behind, between, above, below.
> O, my America, my new-found-land,
> My kingdom, safest when with one man mann'd,
> My mine of precious stones, my empery;
> How am I blest in thus discovering thee!
> To enter in these bonds, is to be free;
> Then, where my hand is set, my soul shall be.

I remember a professor of mine in graduate school telling us, in a seminar on the metaphysical poets, that whenever John

Donne seemed to be talking about sex, he was really talking about God, and when he seemed to be talking about God, he was talking about sex. When he explained that, it felt like we could just close our notebooks and go home. It made life—or at least reading Donne—so much easier. It's often come back to me, sometimes in thinking about Caetano's own body of work—except that I'd be tempted to say: "When it seems like he's talking about sex, he's really talking about politics, and when he seems to be talking about politics, he's talking about sex."[54] I'm joking of course, and so was my professor—none of this is really this easy—but there's an element of truth to it, and in "Elegy XIX," at least, the latter formulation holds even more than the former. "My America, my new-found-land," needless to say, resonates very differently to an American—and here I use the word in its amplest sense, which would include, of course, Caetano. The notion of a colonial "discovery" applies not only to the mines of precious stones, or to the indigenous maiden of "Manhatã," but to Carmen and every other Latin "discovery" claimed by the culture industry. So little surprise that we come back to shamelessness, and nakedness. As Donne continues:

> Full nakedness! All joys are due to thee;
> As souls unbodied, bodies unclothed must be …

Here is the place where it gets a little confusing as to whether Donne is talking about religion or sexuality—when "souls" enter into the equation. If the body is highly present, invoked in the most literal terms in Caetano's songs, what about souls?

What might the soul signify for a confirmed atheist? It's actually a term that arises in his work, sometimes in unexpected ways. There's a cover of the Brazilian pop icon Roberto Carlos's "Fera ferida" ("Wounded Beast," on *Caetano*, 1987) with the refrain, "*Sou fera ferida, no corpo, na alma, e no coração*" (I'm a wounded beast, in my body, my soul, and my heart). I'll say more about pop melodrama and specifically about Roberto Carlos below, but for now, suffice it to say that the invocation of the "soul" in the context of pop romanticism (or a meta-commentary on the social significance of pop romanticism) is not out of reach for Caetano.

But he's invoked the term in other, subtler, or more complex contexts. There's a song called "Clara" (the name of one of his sisters) on his 1968 solo album. By his own estimation, the music on the song is "strange"[55]—an odd, short, slightly rushed cinematic melody, with woodwinds and brass, and the vocal participation of Gal Costa. Most of the words of the song have an open "*a*" sound—"*Calma, alta, clara ...*" (Calm, tall, light ...) A sequence of images follows, all with the open "*a*"—a crowing cock, flowing water ... There's something about white linen in the sun, a white flower, a red carnation, a distant love, and the girl named Clara, Clara, Clara, with her soul in pain ... What's that soul, the soul of a young girl watching white linen drying in the sun, "dying of love"? It's a suspended narrative, melancholy but without a clear cause for pain, something like a character in a story by Clarice Lispector.

And there are other souls, lots of them—"*Tantas almas esticadas no curtume ...*" (So many souls stretched out like hides in a tannery.) This is the stunning image in "O ciúme" ("Jealousy," *Caetano*, 1987). There's a woozy haze, the singer tells us, under a hot sun, and a passing, bleak landscape with just one black spot in focus: his jealousy. He addresses "old Chico"—but the seeming old friend is just a personification of the Rio São Francisco, a "you" who carries everything away and teaches nothing—and the singer is left in utter, irrecuperable solitude. It's an astonishing lyric—an internal, quiet living with the particular form of pain that, ironically, makes one feel most isolated, most alone, even as it proves one to be just like everyone else. One more hide strung up to dry. That's what a soul is.

Cry Me a River / Smoke Gets in Your Eyes

I cried a river over you.
ARTHUR HAMILTON, "CRY ME A RIVER"

Now laughing friends deride
Tears I cannot hide …
OTTO HARBACH AND JEROME KERN, "SMOKE GETS IN YOUR EYES"

Nada serve de chão
onde caiam minhas lágrimas.[56]
CAETANO VELOSO, "MINHAS LÁGRIMAS"

"Old Chico," the river that silently carries everything away, without bothering to teach a person anything about how to handle loss, brings to mind Jerome Kern and Oscar

Hammerstein's "Ol' Man River," from the 1927 Broadway musical *Show Boat*. "Ol' man river … He mus' know sumpin', but don't say nuthin.'" The lyrics of the song are replete not only with vernacular spellings but with racial terms that, over the years, have undergone numerous changes by interpreters. Between the 1936 film version, Paul Robeson's 1938 theatrical revival, and Frank Sinatra's performances of the song from 1946 on, the potentially offending language was watered down from various terms for blackness to an unspecific "we."[57] Actually, in the case of Robeson, "Ol' Man River" isn't "watered down," but rather stirred up: Robeson shifted things such that the black stevedore doesn't envy the river's complacency, but rather resists it. All that to say, the notion of a river of quiet acceptance has served as a political metaphor as well as an affective one.

But in that latter realm, the river of standards, or the standard of rivers, is "Cry Me a River," by Arthur Hamilton. Hamilton wrote it in 1953 for Ella Fitzgerald to sing in a film, but the producers balked over a weird word ("plebeian") and ended up dropping it. Luckily for Hamilton his high school sweetheart, Julie London, liked it,[58] and she recorded it in 1953 with Barney Kessel on guitar and Ray Leatherwood on bass. London reprised it in the film *The Girl Can't Help It* (1956), in which she plays herself as an unforgettable torch singer. And indeed, she's unforgettable, and so is the song. London's rendition is smoky and noir-ish: it opens with Leatherwood's stealthy, footstep-like plucked bass notes, and then Kessel's anxious, furtive guitar, like somebody sticking his head around a corner, looking both ways. Then comes London. If I said that, for me, much of Sinatra's skill as a singer is actually what I'd identify as his skill as an actor, I'd say the same of Julie London. Even before she reprised her performance of this song on screen, she sounded like an actress playing a smoky torch singer. Smoky isn't just a metaphor. In her own words, about her own voice: "It's only a thimbleful of a voice, and I have to use it close to the microphone. But it is a kind of oversmoked voice, and it automatically sounds intimate."[59] Her inhalations are highly audible—it's part of the act, but it's also her lungs. I hope it's clear that to call it an "act" isn't to diminish the genuineness of her performance. On the contrary. Part of the pathos of any torch song is that the narrator is putting up a front. Sometimes calling attention to the front makes it, ironically, sadder.[60]

Caetano's version dispenses with the intro: his voice, the sharp tap of a *tamborim*, a deep plucked bass, and Luiz Brasil's bossa nova guitar enter simultaneously on the first beat: "Now … you say you're lonely." There's a very slight yip on "river," a hint of sass, but as the song progresses, and distant horns enter, any causticness fades. Where London's "*r*"s are hard with sarcasm, his accounting of the heart sounds more like a statement of fact: "I cried a river over you." It's an admission of pain, without drama, rancor, or derision. It's peculiarly blank. Even the reciprocal challenge—your turn to cry—sounds more like a sober description of the state of affairs, or even a mild suggestion, than any kind of execration.

The torch song is, of course, deeply tied to the blues—that is, to African-American singers of both genders—but when damaged or unrequited love was taken up by Tin Pan Alley, it was largely seen as the domain of white women singers—until Frank Sinatra staked a claim on tears.[61] Before that, if crooners—even black crooners—were going to cry, it seems they had to at least give some kind of ironic subterfuge. Maybe the great example of that ploy is Jerome Kern and Otto Harbach's 1933 "Smoke Gets in Your Eyes." It was first recorded by women, but Nat King Cole and Harry Belafonte both recorded versions in the '40s. Even their versions didn't gain publicity until the following decade. By subterfuge, I mean the sly trick of the lyric, which moves undecidably between literal and figurative "smoke" to make an excuse for all-too-real tears. If one's old "flame" is just a flame—of a fire in a fireplace, a candle, or even a cigarette—then one's tears are explained away easily enough: smoke gets in your eyes. Of course it's all too evident what the "lovely flame" really refers to. The version on *A Foreign Sound* begins with an elaborate arrangement of winds, first a harmonic wash of chords, then some slight singular trills and a few blue notes … It's an arrangement that's majestic, but with a wink and a sad smile. Caetano's voice enters, gentlemanly, with just a bit of coyness. But it ends weirdly abruptly, with that little literal/figurative punchline, and then a kind of disoriented little whimper from the horns. Did he just say he was devastated?

Frank Sinatra's 1955 *In the Wee Small Hours* was perhaps the first "break-up album," a genre that's been explored by a wide variety of U.S. recording artists in different styles.[62] *Cê*, the first in Caetano's recent trilogy of alternative rock albums with the Banda Cê, might be framed as a break-up album, and it contains several songs that might be configured as torch songs, among them "Odeio," which I've already mentioned. Two other songs on the album explicitly take up the image of tears, or crying. "*Outro*," like his interpretation of "Cry Me a River," avoids melodrama, even as the narrator acknowledges both producing and provoking tears: "*Eu já chorei muito por você. Também já fiz você chorar.*" (I've cried a lot over you. I also made you cry.) It has that same blank quality, a restrained statement of fact, that I pointed out above in his take on Hamilton's torch song. Despite "*Outro*"'s driving rhythm and the relentlessly repetitive electric guitar and bass lines, it's precisely the restraint of the lyric that gives one a sense of the size of the hole in the narrator's heart. And then there's "*Minhas lágrimas*" ("My Tears"), a slow, tremulous ballad, with its brief, vague description of the view from a plane flying over Los Angeles, over the hazy Pacific, with the wing of the plane in sight, the plane's ugly carpeting, the image of a blank page that can't be filled. Not even writing gives him back a sense of groundedness in the vacuum where love once was. Caetano's voice on the song is as ethereal as the images in it. He cries, that is, but he doesn't exploit his own tears for effect. The affect of these songs isn't exactly flat, but it's vaporous, and numb.

Summertime

Oh, your daddy's rich and your ma is good-lookin'
So hush little baby, don't you cry.

DUBOSE HEYWORD, IRA GERSHWIN, AND GEORGE GERSHWIN,
"SUMMERTIME"

A escravidão permanecerá por muito tempo como a
característica nacional do Brasil.[63]

JOAQUIM NABUCO, *MINHA FORMAÇÃO*

I've already pointed out the peculiar irony of the representation of ethnicity in the American Songbook, and the songs from *Porgy and Bess* are among the most complex examples. George Gershwin wrote the music, with lyrics by DuBose Heyward (author of the original novel and play on which the opera is based) and Ira Gershwin. Of the music, George Gershwin said, confusingly: "I wrote my own spirituals and folksongs. But they are still folk music—and therefore, being in operatic form, *Porgy and Bess* becomes a folk opera."[64] While the lyrics, like those of "Ol' Man River," use vernacular spellings, the opera was conceived, from the outset, to showcase the singing of classically trained African-American singers. Ellen Noonan has detailed the extraordinarily complex reactions that the opera has provoked since its composition in 1934. Noonan's thesis is that the opera fed white Americans' desires for a depiction of both "earthy authenticity" and a "frictionless progress toward racial equality." But she notes that appropriation and racial stereotyping in the work have been recomplicated by the uses made of the songs by both black and white interpreters at various historical junctures. Anxieties—from all sides—tend to turn around the question of authenticity. "It is precisely those attempts to define racial authenticity that make the history of *Porgy and Bess* so revealing of twentieth-century changes in white ideas about African Americans and black ideas about the relationship between cultural representation and political progress."[65] James Baldwin's assessment of the opera—perhaps the most cutting in its perception—was: "It assuages [whites'] guilt about Negroes and it attacks none of their fantasies."[66]

In the first act of *Porgy and Bess*, Clara sings "Summertime" as a lullaby to her baby. It's reprised in the second act, and in the final act Bess sings it to Clara's orphaned child. The first recording was by Abbie Mitchell, accompanied by Gershwin on piano—and it's among the most recorded songs ever.[67] Lyric sopranos like Leontyne Price and Kathleen Battle sang it, as did Billie Holiday, Ella Fitzgerald, Sarah Vaughan, and Nina Simone. Sam Cooke's version is relaxed and silky. The Zombies did it as a lilting rock waltz on their debut album. Janis Joplin's take is a high-pitched, rasping moan. Caetano's version opens with his own beautiful, bluesy, pulled-back but echo-y steel-string guitar. His vocal is in the mode of lullaby—gentle and lovely, with just a hint of keening on the "oh"s. There's no effort at all to replicate the vernacular pronunciations indicated in Heyward and Gershwin's spellings. His phrasing sometimes emphasizes the downbeat, and sometimes draws out an implicit 6/8 running under the 4/4. As with a number of tracks on the album, the ending comes as something of a surprise: with "daddy and mommy" (not mammy) standing by …

The last syllable lands directly on D, the guitar striking that same solitary note, which reverberates for a moment before disappearing—and suddenly it's over. Caetano's "daddy and mommy" ring true, as though the song were really being sung to his children. It's as though he stops because they fell asleep.

If it was a complicated proposition for Gershwin to reference both musical and verbal idioms in attempting to represent, in operatic form, "folk" idioms, Caetano appears to want to allow those complications to fall away, and to "own" the lullaby without staking any claim at all to "authenticity"—or anything one might call "folk art." There's every reason to think he'd be sensitive to the question in a U.S. context, since he's articulated his own concerns about U.S. notions of Brazilian cultural authenticity. In a 2000 essay in the *New York Times*, Caetano expressed some perplexity at North Americans' enthusiasm over French director Marcel Camus's effort, in 1959, to depict black Brazilian "folk" culture in the film *Black Orpheus*. The occasion of Caetano's reflections on Camus's film—and the embrace of it here in the U.S.—was the release of a remake of the story by a Brazilian director, Carlos Diegues. Caetano wrote the score for this film, and it was produced by his partner, Paula Lavigne. The 1999 *Orfeu negro* was an update of the original, incorporating both musical and personal styles (hip-hop, dreadlocks) that more accurately reflected the sounds and looks of contemporary Rio. Some foreign critics decried the modifications of Camus's portrait of "authentic" Brazilian culture. Caetano responded: "We Brazilians are frequently accused of being inauthentic because we don't look enough like whatever foreigners saw in that film. The fact

Standards

83

that Brazilians thoroughly reject the Camus film has been hard for foreigners to accept."[68] He pointed out that Camus's film included strangely out-of-place regional accents, as well as various musical and choreographic inaccuracies. And beyond questions of inaccuracy, Caetano's assessment eerily echoes Baldwin's observations regarding the white reception of *Porgy and Bess*—Camus's film also might be seen as simultaneously guilt-assuaging and titillating.[69]

Caetano's essay goes on to question the scholarly positions of some U.S. "Brazilianists" who have asserted that Brazilians' rejection of Camus's film demonstrates their country's internalized racism—and he further rejects the notion that Brazilians need to learn from the U.S. how to overcome racial prejudice (with its implicit suggestion that this country is exemplary on that score). He defends the Brazilian sociologist Gilberto Freyre who, in the 1930s, published an optimistic account of his country's history of miscegenation (leading to different configurations of racial identity quite distinct from the binaristic U.S. model), promoting an ideal he referred to as "racial democracy."[70] While many U.S. scholars and activists have condemned the phrase as masking the realities (historical and contemporary) of racial discrimination in Brazil, in this essay Caetano continues to find hope in Freyre's formulation.[71]

Some of Caetano's own ideas about the significance of blackness and racial history in Brazil were taken up in his 2000 album, *Noites do Norte*, immediately following his work on Diegues's film. In interviews around the time of the album's release, he didn't link it to his experiences in working on *Orfeu negro.* He referenced instead a book, *Minha formação*, by a nineteenth-century Brazilian abolitionist named Joaquim Nabuco, as a source of inspiration. In fact, the book provides the words to the title track. Caetano set a block of Nabuco's prose to music. It reads in part: "Slavery will remain, for a long time, the national characteristic of Brazil … It left the first imprint on our virgin soil … it breathed into the land its childish spirit, its sadness without substance, its tears without bitterness, its unfocused silence, its random joy and inconsequential happiness."[72] He described the process of finding a musical structure for Nabuco's text on his acoustic guitar:

> When I saw that I had managed to create a musically coherent piece, containing the text with no cuts, I was very pleased, and I already thought that I wanted the orchestra to come in but subjected to a dialog with some heavy percussion, which creates a tension, contrasting with the orchestra. I also wanted the music to have something of the Brazilian seresta as well as classical music of the 19th century, a little connected to opera. I felt a little of the world of Joaquim Nabuco, a 19th-century Brazilian scholar, and something of Brazilian classical music held as nationalistic.[73]

It's quite a grand stake to claim: dialogical, century-spanning, classical. It's certainly different from Gershwin's operatic representation of racial tropes, but it's interesting to hold them side by side.

When *Noites do Norte* was released here, music critics tended to laud the musical mix of samba, hip-hop, rock, and

Jaques Morelenbaum's lush orchestrations (indeed, in the case of the title track, operatic)—and they also seemed open to the challenges that the lyrical content presented to limited U.S. conceptions of racial history.[74] But some scholars of comparative race relations in the Americas pushed back against what they perceived as yet another romantic account of that history in Brazil.[75] *Noites do Norte* is, to me, a complex, sometimes gorgeous, sometimes perturbing album. In fact, some of my own perturbation comes at its moments of greatest beauty. But it's a more complex proposition than a simple sentimentalizing of the history of exploitation of black Brazilians. The CD was accompanied by gorgeous and potentially troubling images—Mario Cravo Neto's photographs of black Brazilians reclining, embracing, or posing with cool indifference on the beach. The young men are draped in gold chains, toqued in knit caps, eyes obscured by wrap-around mirrored sunglasses: the accouterments associated with hip-hop style. There's a languorous eroticism in these photographs that might invite comparison to Robert Mapplethorpe's images in *Black Book*.[76]

Caetano wrote in the liner notes for the U.S. version of the album that, while he was stirred by his reading of Nabuco, *Noites do Norte* didn't begin with a thematic vision. "I went to the studio looking for sounds …" On the first track, "I decided to record first the drums and put the guitar on top. I called Cleber [Sena], who is the drummer of the band Afro Reggae, from the Vigário Geral slum, which plays hip-hop. At the time he was 16 years old. I wanted to place a bossa nova / samba guitar on top of the hip-hop." Given his comments in the *Times* about the authenticity of hip-hop in contemporary Brazilian music, it seems likely that the swirl of musical idioms was as important to his meditations on a "nationalistic" sound as Nabuco's reflections on the reverberations of slave history. In fact, one thing is inextricable from the other. In an interview, he described the experience of working with the young percussionists on the album: "They have a vision of race that is new for Brazil. They're identifying themselves as a precise group, and in hip-hop they find a racial affirmation. That is tremendously important, because for years there hasn't been any discussion of race—the very notion that I picked that piece from Nabuco was much discussed in the academy and among militants."[77] How does one reconcile this with his rejection of the notion that a U.S. model of racial identity should serve as a model for Brazilians? Somehow, both positions co-exist, not only in Caetano's pronouncements about the album, but also in its sound.

The Nabuco track is followed by two other tracks that continue to plumb the question of how black history in Brazil might be represented musically.[78] "13 de Maio" is a samba in 5/4.[79] It's an hommage to Princess Isabel, who was long celebrated for signing the "Golden Law" that abolished slavery. The lyrics recall the fireworks in the market square of Santo Amaro, Bahia, where Caetano was born. Every May 13 in his youth, "os pretos celebravam (talvez hoje ainda o façam) o fim da escravidão ... Foguetes no ar pra saudar Isabel ..." (The blacks celebrated [maybe they still do today] the end of slavery ... Fireworks in the air to salute Isabel ...) In his track notes for the CD on the Nonesuch website,[80] Caetano actually answers the question of whether the party's changed: the festivities still exist, he says, but since the 1970s, "greatly influenced by the North American black movement," the community has shifted its focus from Princess Isabel to a celebration of Zumbi, the legendary leader of a great settlement of rebel slaves. "Princess Isabel's candle was put out. I agree totally with the elevation of Zumbi to this place, but I always liked Princess Isabel, and … I wanted to write a song about" the celebrations she once inspired. Still, this track is followed immediately by—precisely—"Zumbi," a composition by his contemporary Jorge Ben. He recounts his sense of astonishment on first hearing the song in the 1970s. It wasn't merely Jorge Ben's radically original stylistic fusion of R&B with samba—it was also his lyrics: "'Here where the men are'—that was a way to put things! There are also sentences that seem like they were taken out of history books, names of countries, from where the Africans were imported to be enslaved … Then repeated: 'I just want to see, I just want to see, I just want to see, when Zumbi arrives.' When he said this, what a marvelous thing. I climbed on stage and placed my head at the feet of Jorge Ben. This placement of the possibility of the arrival of Zumbi in the future … This is a beautiful thing, because Zumbi has not arrived yet, slavery did not go away yet, abolition has not finished."

Of course, it isn't finished here either. And for all that Caetano has questioned the imposition of a U.S. perspective on racial identity and race politics, his vision of a "nationalistic" Brazilian sound includes artists—from the 1970s and from the current scene—who were profoundly impacted by certain U.S. models of both black musicality and black politicization. Well, he was too, though he's constantly pressed for the impact to be dialogical, not imposed. And the mixity of the sound, with its political traces, is as important to his notion of an "operatic" representation of Brazil as samba, bossa, cool jazz, and rock.

Jamaica Farewell

But I'm sad to say I'm on my way,
Won't be back for many a day.
LORD BURGESS, "JAMAICA FAREWELL"

O Haiti é aqui,
O Haiti não é aqui.[81]
CAETANO VELOSO, "HAITI"

Harry Belafonte recorded "Jamaica Farewell" on his hugely popular *Calypso* album in 1957. The song isn't actually a calypso—it's (sort of) a mento, which is a Jamaican form distinct from the calypso of Trinidad and Tobago. But, as with "Summertime," the question of the cultural accuracy or authenticity of "Jamaica Farewell" is pretty complicated. The composition is credited to Lord Burgess (Irving Burgie), though Burgess acknowledged that the song was largely pieced together from some traditional material. Burgess, who wrote most of the tracks on *Calypso*, was the Brooklyn-born son of a Barbadian mother. Harry Belafonte was the Harlem-born son of a Jamaican mother and a (Jamaican-born) Martinican father, though he spent much of his childhood living with his grandmother in Jamaica. When the "calypso craze" hit here in the U.S., Belafonte was hailed as the "King of Calypso"—a moniker he himself protested, because there was actually an official "Calypso Monarchy" in Trinidad—a competition, open only to Trinidadians, annually crowning a King for producing the best song in the genre for that year's carnival. Belafonte, of course, was never in the running. Geoffrey Holder, for one, was irked by Belafonte's mantle, and by a craze he considered rife with cultural imprecision. He published a piece in the *New York Times* pointing out that "true" calypso was a raw, improvisational form, unlike "Manhattan calypso," a "slicked up, prettied up, and sophisticated up" vague approximation. "Also," Holder noted, the U.S. version "must more nearly conform to the popular music Americans know than to the West Indian music they don't know."[82] Maybe this sounds familiar. Indeed, if you listen to Belafonte's version of "Jamaica Farewell," you would possibly describe it as slick—and you would certainly describe it as pretty and sophisticated—in fact, *very* pretty and sophisticated! And though it's included on an album called *Calypso*, it's not a calypso. Which indicates, unsurprisingly, that the "calypso craze" didn't indicate a desire on the part of U.S. listeners to attend to the specificities of distinct Caribbean cultures and histories. The performance scholar Shane Vogel, however, argues that the black American artists involved in the production of that "craze" were not merely appropriating and misrepresenting Caribbean music, but were availing themselves of a popular island fantasy in order to enact what he calls a "mock transnational performance ... tak[ing] up the misuse of diasporic cultural indices to critique and refigure the politics of the nation-state and racialized national formations."[83] "Manhattan calypso," that is, provided a place to pose alternative visions of what could constitute blackness in this country, and beyond.

Other people have recorded "Jamaica Farewell": Sam Cooke, The Beach Boys (unreleased), Jimmy Buffett, Sting, Dan Zanes and Angélique Kidjo, Carly Simon—but Belafonte's version remains definitive. Caetano's version might also be described as somewhat slick, very pretty, and very sophisticated. On the first verse, he's accompanied only by a serene, refined duo of acoustic guitars, both classical and steel-string. Caetano's diction is pure, his phrasing delicate—his inhalations are light and specific, buoyant, syncopated—but the sustained notes have a debonair vibrato. He maintains the vocal style even when, in the second verse, the percussion enters. I've already referenced Caetano's use, on this and other albums, of Brazilian street percussion forms.[84] Numerous musicologists and cultural critics, both in and outside of Brazil, have considered the significance of the development, since the 1970s, of Brazilian rhythms and musical styles that merge the ostensible "national" rhythm—samba—with those of the rest of the African diaspora. Gerard Béhague offers a compressed analysis of this turn: "instead of simply assimilating outside influences into a local genre or movement, the presence of foreign genres is acknowledged as part of the local scene: samba-rock, samba-reggae, samba-rap. But this acknowledgement does not imply mere imitation of the foreign models or, for that matter, passive consumption by national audiences." Béhague finds the case of samba-reggae (a rhythm, as I noted above, popularized by the Afrocentric

Bahian carnival group Olodum in the 1980s) particularly telling: "Traditionally, Bahia never had direct contacts or connections with Jamaica, but in their own activist ideology of black exaltation, the young *bloco afro* musicians naturally recognized symbolic models of contemporary black consciousness: themes of the U.S. African-American civil rights movement and the Black Soul movement, and especially the Jamaican independence movement since the 1960s and its messages in reggae and Rastafarianism."[85] The popularity of reggae in Brazil, he argues, was not manufactured or manipulated by the transnational music industry, but expressed a local desire to find global (and historical) connections with communities facing parallel political struggles. And, rather than passively consuming Jamaican sounds, these musicians incorporated them into their own music, explicitly calling attention to those political parallels both in their lyrics and in the groups' public pronouncements. This analysis is of course quite close to Caetano's observations in the notes for *Noites do Norte*.

Seven years before *Noites do Norte*, in 1993, Caetano and Gil released *Tropicália 2*, an album celebrating the twenty-fifth anniversary of their collaboration as well as their involvement in the late-1960s *tropicália* movement. Their album included "Haiti" (with words by Caetano, the music co-authored by Gil[86]), a song that deservedly received a great deal of attention. In fact, I myself took the lyric as a kind of rhizomatic map for a book I was writing about the spread of diasporic culture and political discourse.[87] "Haiti"'s non-linear narrative opens in a carnival square in Bahia, where the percussive slap of hands and sticks on drumheads mixes with the literal violence of the military police attacking the "black riff-raff." Caetano performs the song as a recitative—or, if you prefer, a rap. And that's part of the point—the invocation of another insurrectionary diasporic musical style in a song about race-based violence in Brazil. There's more to the lyric: it touches on the touristic refurbishment of that Bahian plaza for international pleasure-seekers, national TV coverage on a show called *Fantástico*, Paul Simon's record release— and also: economic policies that maintain class disparities, governmental hypocrisy and corruption, oppressive religious dictates that value the life of a fetus over that of a petty criminal, and the 1993 massacre of 111 unarmed (and mostly black) prisoners in Carandiru, São Paulo's House of Detention. Finally, there's a direct address to the listener, who's instructed, on his next Caribbean adventure in sex tourism, to keep Haiti in his prayers.

"How," I asked, listening to that lyric, "have we moved so quickly from the ecstatic crackling of drums, an irresistible, celebratory rhythm that marks itself as simultaneously Afrocentric and diasporic, to the bloody scene at the House of Detention?" Caetano's rap rises to that fevered pitch before lifting off into an airy, suspended refrain: "*O Haiti é aqui ... O Haiti não é aqui ...* " (Haiti is here. Haiti isn't here.)

In my book I pointed out that, in his compressed lyricism, Caetano had managed to spin together "economic, sexual and political exploitation, AIDS, and the pounding of drums, all through the politically charged musical idiom of rap, which is then layered over the already syncretic and markedly diasporic rhythm of samba-reggae. In other words, Haiti is here—you could be in Port-au-Prince—but so could you be in LA, in Kingston, in Havana, in Lagos."[88] There's one thing I didn't point out, however, in that reading. When he comes to the ethereal refrain "*O Haiti é aqui ...*" there's both a lyrical and a musical echo of a dreamy, paradisiacal line from "Menino do Rio": "*O Havaí seja aqui ...*" (Let Hawaii be here ...) It was a gentle, slightly comical suggestion in that earlier song, as though the sun, sand, and surf of Ipanema weren't enough: let's imagine we're on Waikiki. Hawaii was and wasn't there—that is, both tropical paradises were simultaneously real and imagined, colonized, and eternalized in pop iconography.[89] But Haiti (which, for all of its beauty, occupies a very different place in the global imaginary[90]) also was and wasn't, is and isn't there—and here.

Blue Skies / Something Good

Blue skies
Smiling at me.
IRVING BERLIN

Céu azul que vem até onde os pés
Tocam a terra ...[91]
CAETANO VELOSO, "LUZ DO SOL"

Somewhere in my youth or childhood,
I must have done something good.
RICHARD RODGERS

Venha conhecer a vida.
Eu digo que ela é gostosa![92]
CAETANO VELOSO, "BOAS VINDAS"

What about joy?

Caetano's version of "Blue Skies" opens peculiarly with an eerie electronic buzz, a slightly anxiety-producing percussive tapping, more futuristic zaps and pings, and then a humming hive of cellos, before these elements organize themselves into a somewhat more conventional orchestral arrangement topped with the continued tapping and zapping of a collection of traditional and unconventional instruments and noisemakers. The arrangement is Morelenbaum's, but the extensive list of everything besides the cellos is attributed to Carlinhos Brown.[93] While the cello ensemble creates a stately base, Brown's scattershot, acoustic/electronic polyrhythmic insertions sometimes introduce a faint, almost military echo of those street percussion sounds we've already encountered, and sometimes ping you into what feels like a very abstracted cyberspace.[94] And over that strange texture, layering multiple locations and times, floats Caetano's supremely tranquil voice.

Sort of like a bluebird, singin' a song.

In contrast to this tranquility, "Blue Skies" is often interpreted with an almost manic cheer. In fact, Irving Berlin composed "Blue Skies" in one manic night, at the request of Belle Baker, who was about to make her Broadway debut in the Rodgers and Hart musical *Betsy*. Baker (née Becker) was a Vaudeville headliner with a Yiddish-themed act. *Betsy* was intended to showcase Baker's belting capacities, but she didn't really think there was a show-stopper in the score, so she got Berlin to contribute a song at the last minute. It was, even Rodgers had to concede,[95] the one keeper in the show. *Betsy* turned out to be a flop, but Berlin's song remained. The next year, Al Jolson sang it in *The Jazz Singer*. In the film, he plays it on the piano for his doting mother. Though Jolson's not in blackface, he makes all the hammy faces of his theatrical act, and then leans in and says, "You like that mama? I'm glad of it, I'd rather please you than anybody I know of!" There's more tender cajoling and caressing between them until Jakie's father, the Jewish cantor, arrives to express his chagrin over the shenanigans. *The Jazz Singer* was the first feature-length talkie, and plenty of people have weighed in on the implications of its story of Jewish appropriation of blackness.[96] Strangely, both the song's origins in a Yiddish-inflected musical flop and its swerve through a cinematic representation of blackface seem to have been largely elided with the years—much in the way that the opening strophe of the lyric (a little preamble about cloudy days) has largely been elided from recordings. Caetano elides it as well.

He opens directly on blue skies. Blue—*azul*—is a color which references seemingly opposed emotional states in English. The song "Blue Skies" itself has helped to affix a connotation of pure joy to the color in our minds—but that elided first verse also makes direct reference to being blue in quite the opposite sense. Dictionaries will tell you that "blue" in the sense of "sad" probably derives from a seventeenth-century British name for depression, or more specifically, the discomfort provoked by alcohol withdrawal: the "blue devils." And it's likely that the same trail led to the naming of the genre of melancholy African-American song as the blues—and further, to the naming of microtonally flatted or bent notes as "blue notes."[97] In Brazilian Portuguese, if you say everything's blue—*tudo azul*—it's to say everything's copacetic—joyous! It seems likely that the grounds for that are (and I mean here for grounds to evoke also the literal ground), ironically, the sky. But that's not to say that things can't be *tudo azul* without a trace of the blues—that is, without a sense of weighty groundedness.

Caetano's own "Luz do sol" ("Sunlight") begins, also, in full light—literally and figuratively. That is, in both of his recorded versions of the song,[98] the opening phrase "Sunlight!" strikes, soaringly, with the first strummed chord, directly on the first beat, directly on the tonic. The light filters down, with the melody, descending through chord changes and through the leaves, which take and "translate" it into new growth, something verdant, fertile, fresh. And then suddenly (think photosynthesis), he's soaring back up again in the second strophe: "Blue sky!"—that also descends—"to the place where our feet touch the earth," where green nature exhales its circular blue notes. The (musical) bridge extends across a river, the river extends toward the sea, and alongside it, walking, the singer recognizes a human figure, coursing that troubled ground, carrying his own burning wound. It's an image of pain, but the bridge presses gently forward, encouragingly, as if to say: keep marching, you'll leave your blues behind like footprints in the soil. And then he's soaring again: "Sunlight!"

To say, as he does, that the earth "exhales its blues" is a peculiar rhetorical configuration in Portuguese, which doesn't colloquially include a sense of a person's or—stranger still—a *thing's* "blues" as his, her, or *its* sorrow. The song isn't written as a blues. But the blues are somewhere in it, that is, in the understanding of the very purpose of the blues, an exhalation that translates pain—individual, racial, perhaps even cosmic—into song that somehow sustains. And ironically, the earth's blues—"*seus azuis*"—is a homophone for *céus azuis*. Blue Skies.

But the blues isn't the only musical genre to take on the question of transforming pain into pleasure. In "Samba da benção," Vinícius de Moraes gave a kind of primer on how to write samba lyrics: "*prá fazer um samba com beleza, é preciso um bocado de tristeza*" (to make a beautiful samba, you have to have a mouthful of sadness). The song ends with Moraes expressly acknowledging that the insight into samba's alchemical capacity to change pain to pleasure has something to do with its racial history: he says that even if samba, today, is the domain of white poets, it's at its heart black as can be. Of course, the "if" in that proposition should give one pause. There were, and are, plenty of black poets in the history of samba who also laid bare the possibilities of finding pleasure in the transformation of pain into music.[99] And there was also João Gilberto, who managed, in his abstracted interpretations of even the most apparently exultant sambas, to find some secreted sadness. When you listen to him, your task is the inverse: to hear the implicit ecstatic crackle of joy behind his bare whisper of a voice, and his guitar's tracing-paper sketch of the polyrhythms of a massive, exuberant percussion ensemble.

On *A Foreign Sound*, "Blue Skies" immediately follows one other apparent song of explicit joy—"Something Good," which was written by Richard Rodgers for the film version of *The Sound of Music* in 1965 (he and Hammerstein had written the music for the staged version, but Rodgers wrote this one for the screen, replacing a number that wasn't quite working). Although it was hugely popular with audiences (it broke all kinds of box office records), the film opened to mixed—in fact mostly horrible—reviews. Critics all seemed to resort to metaphors of syrup and sap. Judith Crist titled her review in the *New York Herald Tribune*, "If You Have Diabetes, Stay Away from This Movie." She called the general aesthetic "icky-sticky." In *McCall's*, Pauline Kael bemoaned audiences' capacity to swallow so much treacle, particularly in relation to a film ostensibly depicting historical realities: "The Sound of Music is the sugar-coated lie that people seem to want to eat."[100]

And, indeed, in the film, Julie Andrews delivers the lyric with, to invoke that other on-screen persona she appears to be practically reprising, more than a spoonful of sugar. Maria is ostensibly a little more sensually inclined than Mary Poppins, but what counts as naughtiness for a nun-in-training isn't, um, all that bad. So when she sings of her possible "wicked, miserable past," you take it (to extend the metaphor of seasoning, sorry) with a grain of salt. Andrews's singing begins somewhat hushed and confessional, with audible, nearly voiced inhalations, and her inflections on "I must have done something good" have all the treacly, goody-two-shoes earnestness of the strings behind her.

Caetano's version is also hushed, but of a very different character. For one thing, he is not, nor has he ever been, a nun. But that's not to say that his interpretation is insincere. He's accompanied only by his own acoustic guitar, and while he doesn't play it in the rhythmic style of bossa nova, the spareness of his playing and the intimacy of his vocal evoke João. The plosives are wet. So are the "*k*"s. His "wicked" isn't the jokey "wicked wacky wicky" of "The Carioca," nor the "icky-sticky" of Julie Andrews—it's shy, confidential, and strangely vulnerable. There's a bit of a wobble, something genuinely abashed about the line that marvels at the lover's having materialized. The ending slows, he comes to that final, bewildered "I must have done something good," and the palatalized "d" hangs there for a few seconds in the silence, like a question mark. It's certainly nakeder than Andrews's, and naughtier. Needless to say, it's also sexier.

There's another song in his own repertoire that expresses a kind of heartfelt—and yet also sexy—joy: "Boas Vindas" ("Welcome," on *Circuladô*, 1991). The song is familial, and it's a samba. That is, it's a family affair, with his first son, Moreno, among the clapping hands that create the intimate, domestic sound of *samba de roda*.[101] The song anticipated the birth of Caetano's second son, Zeca—the first child of his second marriage—and the lyric enumerates those waiting to welcome him: his mother and dad, his brother, his brother's mother … The list goes on—it's a "blended family,"[102] but everybody's on board to welcome the baby. "*Venha conhecer a vida! … Eu digo que ela é gostosa!* (Come meet life! … I say it's delicious! I say she's delicious!) I translate that line (which is repeated, and in fact modulates) two ways, because they're both implicit in it. That is, life, and the joyous embrace of a complex, intentional family, *is* sexy. So is the expectant mother. Life is complicated, but it's delicious. Sweet, but not treacly. Sexy.

Nature Boy

How beautiful
Could a being be?
MORENO VELOSO, "HOW BEAUTIFUL COULD A BEING BE?"

There was a boy,
A very strange enchanted boy …
EDEN AHBEZ, "NATURE BOY"

But perhaps the purest expression of joy in Caetano's discography is a song composed by Moreno Veloso, the older son,[103] who arranged "13 de Maio" and who participated in the clapping chorus of "Boas Vindas." Caetano recorded Moreno's "How Beautiful Could a Being Be?" on *Livro*. Moreno also sings on the track. Once again, it's a domestic, cozy and spontaneous-sounding samba.[104] A voice enters in high falsetto—to tell the truth, I'm not sure if it's Moreno's or Caetano's. In this very high range, their voices are barely distinguishable. That first line comes in slowly, floating like an extended sigh. And then the two of them pick up the rhythm, alternating, repeating, over and over, the question that the song itself seems to answer: How beautiful could a being be? So simple! It's a little descending run of notes, with a trip step in the middle, and then the choral refrain: "Could a being be? Could a being be?" The electric guitar comes in to noodle a little on three notes, and it all starts up again, with friends and familiars clapping in syncopation, filling out the refrain. Finally, there's no choice but to let the song fade out. But you don't want it to end. Three minutes and twenty-eight seconds of pure joy.

The first time Moreno recorded with Caetano, it was 1982, when he was ten years old. "Um Canto de Afoxé" (*Cores, Nomes*, Philips) was composed by the two of them, father and son, and it's a tribute to the Afrocentric Bahian carnival group, Ilê Aiyê. "*Ilê Aiyê, como você é bonito de se ver … Que beleza mais bonita de se ter …*" (Ile Aiyê, how beautiful you are to see … What a beauteous beauty to behold …) It's a childlike lyric, which is, of course, its charm. If you look on YouTube, you can find them singing it together on stage in 1982. Moreno appears to be—a very strange enchanted boy. His music is still strange and enchanting.[105]

Which perhaps explains, at least in part, why Caetano dedicated the track "Nature Boy" to Moreno on *A Foreign Sound*. There was a boy, a very strange enchanted boy … The adoption of "Nature Boy" in the American Songbook is itself a particularly strange story. It was written in 1947 by eden ahbez (né George Alexander Aberle), Brooklyn Jew turned eccentric proto-hippie and vegan, who moved to Los Angeles and slept outdoors (reputedly under an "L" in the Hollywood Sign). ahbez slipped the sheet music for the song to Nat King Cole via his personal valet after a show, and, remarkably, Cole decided to perform and then record it. It took a while for the record executives to track ahbez down, but they did, and he gave his permission. It reached #1 on the *Billboard* chart, and vastly expanded Cole's audience. There were some legal complications—Herman Yablokoff sued ahbez, claiming that the melody had been lifted from his "*Shvayg mayn harts*" which he'd written for a Yiddish theater piece. ahbez insisted the tune had been delivered to him as if by angels, but he settled out of court with Yablokoff. (Others have noted a different possible musical source: Antonín Dvořák's Piano Quintet No. 2). There were also subsequent legal disputes over the arrangement with the American Federation of Musicians. In the words of Will Friedwald, "it struck no one as ironic that a song with a message of love and peace should come to symbolize how cutthroat the pop music business was becoming."[106] There have been many covers: Frank Sinatra, Dick Haymes, Bobby Darin, Sarah Vaughan, Grace Slick, Ella Fitzgerald, Abbey Lincoln—also David Bowie (for the soundtrack of the film *Moulin Rouge*), Celine Dion, Aaron Neville—and most recently Lady Gaga and Tony Bennett. Gaga tweeted enthusiastically, "This composer was part of a sub-culture of nomadic hippies!"[107] But for many interpreters, the hommage seems to be less about ahbez and more about Nat King Cole.

Caetano mentions Cole early in his memoir, explaining that, while he listened to him (and other U.S. practitioners of jazz, soul, and incipient rock 'n' roll) in his adolescence, he and his friends were resistant to the way in which some young Brazilians were unquestioningly mimicking U.S. artists. "It wasn't that my friends and I found those who did [this] 'culturally inauthentic,' or even alienated from our national or regional roots ... Rather, what we found objectionable—without yet being quite able to say it this way—was that these kids were imitating a dazzling style that had come at them without their knowing what it meant."[108] That mimicry was largely taking place in the idiom of rock, which I'll address in the subsequent chapters. But "Nature Boy" is a fascinating song in that it shows just how weirdly the boundaries can blur both between communities and between musical idioms. Possibly a Yiddish theater tune (with a trace of Dvořák), reconfigured by a California proto-hippie vegan with long blond hair, a flowing beard, a white tunic, and sandals—recorded by an elegant jazz pianist who would, in part through that song, become ensconced as the first black crooner, reaching a wider audience, though also incurring some accusations of "selling out" in the process. ahbez would go on to write songs for Eartha Kitt and Frankie Laine, but later he'd consort with Brian Wilson and Donovan, seeming kindred spirits.

Though all of these ironies speak to interests of Caetano's—his music is similarly impossible to pigeonhole—I think maybe the appeal of the song for him is quite personal: it makes him think of his son. He'd recorded it before (a live version, with just his own acoustic guitar, appears on *Totalmente Demais*, 1986). But the version on *A Foreign Sound* is arranged by Pedro Sá,[109] who plays an eerie filigree of electric guitars (sustained and fuzzy, echo-y, tinkling). It's an uncanny canvas for Caetano's voice, which is meditative, gentle, and very careful. The vowels are stretched, and sometimes have that aspirated quality I've spoken of. He sings it just once through, and the track fades out with the faint sound of an electric amp's buzz.

Different people have interpreted the "love" in "Nature Boy" in different ways, from supernatural to homoerotic to garden-variety romantic. Caetano's version is a love song from a father to his son. ahbez's close friend Joe Romersa says that ahbez wasn't entirely satisfied with the way he'd written about love in "Nature Boy." "He said to me, 'Joe, that lyric, "To love and be loved in return" … it's too much of a deal. There's no deal in love.'"[110] It seems he wished he'd ended it: "The greatest thing you'll ever learn is to love and be loved, just to love and be loved." But it didn't fit the melody.[111]

Maybe that sounds like a proto-hippie espousal of free love, though by all accounts ahbez was extremely dedicated to his wife, Anna, until her death. His promiscuity, if one were inclined to use such a word, was musical, and the song he's remembered for appears to have encouraged (or appealed to) a kind of *musical* ethos of free love in various artists—a crossing of various boundaries. That ethos has been in Caetano's music from the get-go, though never in a naïve way. In fact, Caetano's love of foreign sounds can often have an undercurrent of resistance. If Moreno taught him something, I suspect it may be to *sometimes* allow that love to be innocent. Just to love and be loved.

Notes

1   "Look what a beautiful thing, so graceful, it's her, the girl who approaches and passes …"

2   Thomas Vinciguerra, "The Elusive Girl from Ipanema: The

endlessly covered Brazilian song turns 50 this year. What explains its quirky endurance?" *Wall Street Journal* (online), July 2, 2012.

3 Critiques of Astrud Gilberto's singing on the recording aren't uncommon, and they're always overstated—in fact, wrong. Vinciguerra calls her delivery "unpolished," but Ruy Castro (*Bossa Nova*: 257) debunks the myth of Astrud's "incidental" or amateurish participation on the album, arguing that she and João had been working for some time on her vocal technique, which in fact shows plenty of nuance—and the clear mark of João's influence in both tone and phrasing. An ostensible lack of technical proficiency is also part of the myth of João, who made an ironic nod to his purported "tunelessness" on "Desafinado" (also on *Getz/Gilberto*).

4 See Introduction, note 11.

5 It's also not the only purportedly "Brazilian" dance form modified (even arguably invented), propagated, and eventually abandoned by outsiders: the short-lived *lambada* craze of the '80s swelled—and rapidly deflated— around a song with Bolivian folkloric origins interpreted by a mostly Senegalese pop band backed by some wily French promoters. When that craze started, I myself had a very brief stint as one of the official Palladium *lambada* dancers in New York—and was also there just months later when everybody was so sick of the over-promoted "forbidden dance" that they held a *lambada* record-smashing party—that is, we literally stomped on the vinyls.

6 That trio appears as a Hollywood rendering of the various racial "flavors" of Brazil.

7 The timbau has a very particular resonance: it's a conical drum similar to the *atabaque* drums played in Afro-Brazilian religious music, and, like them, it's struck with the hands. The instrument became a staple of popular music in the early '90s, when Carlinhos Brown founded the band and carnival organization Timbalada. Early in his career, Brown performed with Caetano as a percussionist, and Caetano recorded a composition of Brown's "Meia Lua Inteira" on *Estrangeiro*. Brown has gone on to have a high-profile career as a singer, composer, band-leader, and community activist. Timbalada is one of a number of Bahian percussion ensembles that achieved both national and international prominence in the '80s and '90s. The carnival group Olodum, which plays a rhythm called samba-reggae, was particularly visible, appearing in music videos (and playing on recordings) of Michael Jackson and Paul Simon, among others—another moment of intense Brazilian influence in the U.S. popular music sphere. See Larry Crook, *Focus: Music of Northeastern* Brazil (Routledge, New York, 2009, p. 224).

8 "Goddess of the legend on the prow, she lifts a torch in her hand."

9 I write this in the winter of 2016, as presidential politicking has raised the anti-immigration rhetoric of some candidates to baffling—and deeply dispiriting—levels.

10 *Sobre as Letras*, 46–7. Caetano told me that when Lulu Santos had first uttered the island's name to him, with that Brazilianized pronunciation, he thought it was Lulu's own invention. But later, Lulu explained that he'd been referring to a 1988 song, also titled "Manhatã," by Cazuza and Leoni—a song narrated by a Brazilian living in Manhattan speaking bad English, mispronouncing things but feeling like the king of the world: "E até garçon me chama de sir / Oh! Baby, baby, só vendo pra crer!" (Even the waiter calls me 'sir' / Oh! Baby, baby, you have to see it to believe it!)

11   This is precisely the mix that marks a number of tracks on *A Foreign Sound*, though not "Manhattan," which I'll get to in short order …

12   Ben Ratliff, "JAZZ FESTIVAL REVIEW; Wily Mixer Of Cool Jazz, Brazilian Pop And High Art," *New York Times*, June 29, 1999. http://www.nytimes.com/1999/06/29/arts/jazz-festival-review-wily-mixer-of-cool-jazz-brazilian-pop-and-high-art.html (accessed 19 March 2017).

13   *Songs for Any Taste*, 1957.

14   One can only guess the tongue-in-cheek rhyme Hart might have inserted here if he were writing the lyric today.

15   http://positiveanymore.blogspot.com/2006/04/how-you-sound.html (accessed 19 March 2017).

16   When he bought an apartment in Manhattan some years ago, it was, indeed, on the Lower East Side, and he shared it with his partner Paula Lavigne—meaning the lyrics of the song, in a sense, fit like a glove. Their periodic domestic experiences in New York in the '90s are part of the background on "Manhatã," where you can faintly hear Caetano practicing the pronunciation of the word "stroller," which is presumably an apparatus he and Lavigne were maneuvering around the city sidewalks with their kids. The question of ethnic identification, though, goes beyond his domestic life. Caetano has made any number of public statements regarding his longtime sense of connection to Jewish culture, from his early encounter as a student with the writings of Sartre until the present.

17 http://www.pbs.org/wnet/gperf/broadway-musicals-a-jewish-legacy-about-the-film/1476/ (accessed 19 March 2017). Porter's biographers and musicologists alike have made similar claims. See Charles Schwartz, *Cole Porter: A Biography* (DaCapo Press, 1979, pp. 231–2) and Jack Gottlieb, *Funny, It Doesn't Sound Jewish: How Yiddish Songs and Synagogue Melodies Influenced Tin Pan Alley, Broadway, and Hollywood* (SUNY Press, Albany, NY, 2004, 191), which both make special reference to "So in Love," discussed below. Porter's attitude toward Jewish ethnicity has been interpreted variously as Judeophilic or (as Schwartz puts it) "verging on" Judeophobia. On the general question of the prevalence of Jewish composers in the American Songbook, see also David Lehman, *A Fine Romance: Jewish Songwriters, American Songs* (Schocken, New York, 2009).

18 It's exceeded in simplicity only by the *a cappella* "Love for Sale," which I discuss below.

19 On *Once Upon a Summertime* (Verve, 1959).

20 "I know I'll love you / For all my life I'll love you …"

21 "I only ask that you accept / My strange love."

22 Benjamin Sears, ed., *Irving Berlin Reader* (Oxford University Press, New York, 2012), p. 80.

23 It appears on both *Muito* and his 1986 eponymous album, each time opening with a fragment of Jobim and Aloysio de Oliveira's bossa standard, "Dindi."

24 She notes the complex gender relations inscribed in popular song from eighteenth-century *modinhas* through early twentieth-century *samba-canção* to bossa nova and rock-inflected *iê-iê-iê* (Leu, 103–19).

25 Leu, 124-145.

26 She considers, for example, a trio of songs from *Muito* ("Muito romântico," "Como dois e dois," and "Força estranha"), paying hommage to the Brazilian pop rock star Roberto Carlos (whom I discuss below), and which address the power of music to shake up a stagnant social sphere. Social critique would similarly appear to be the central concerns of "O quereres" (*Velô*, 1984) and "Eu sou neguinha?" (*Caetano*, 1987), also analyzed by Leu as "love songs."

27 *"Jaquinho e eu reforçamos as semelhanças com 'Você é linda' porque achamos graciosa a ilusão de que eu tenho um estilo próprio de canção de amor." O mundo não é chato*, 176.

28 At the time, he was married to Dedé Gadelha.

29 Pedro Sá (electric guitar), Marcelo Callado (drums), and Ricardo Dias Gomes (bass).

30 Leu, 134.

31 The series also included two albums dedicated to Brazilian music, *Red Hot + Rio* (1996) and *Red Hot +Rio 2* (2011)— both of which included tracks by Caetano. The latter also included covers of several of his compositions by other artists.

32 Lori Burns, "Genre, Gender, and Convention Revisited: k.d. lang's Cover of Cole Porter's 'So in Love.'" Repercussions 7–8, 1999–2000, 299–325 (299).

33 The battle to end all battles between the sexes: *The Taming of the Shrew*. In the film version, it's only sung once, and Lilli and Fred alternate lines.

34 Jet, as in the stone, or color.

35 On *Totalmente Demais* (1986).

36 Bennett's version is vaguely "tropical"; both Tormé's and Connick's versions are upbeat and swinging—as is the version Tormé's son James recorded in 2011 (James Tormé also altered the lyrics). Connick's cover may be rhythmically buoyant, but it's not comical, nor does it seem to give much wistful weight to the story. Rather, it appears to serve him, precisely, as a standard: a highly recognizable melody through which to showcase his jazz chops, without, I'm hazarding, much emphasis on the lyric content.

37 There is a fairly extensive bibliography on gender transgression in Brazilian popular music since the 1960s, much of it focussing on female narrators in compositions by Chico Buarque, Gil's philosophical reflections on gender fusion, and Caetano's complex articulations of sex and sexuality. See, for example, Perrone, *Masters of Contemporary Brazilian Song: MPB 1965–1985* (1993) and Dunn, *Brutality Garden* (2001). See also César Braga-Pinto, "Supermen and Chiquita Bacana's Daughters: Transgendered Voices in Brazilian Popular Music," in *Lusosex: Gender and Sexuality in the Portuguese Speaking World*, ed.

Susan Canty Quinlan and Fernando Arenas (University of Minnesota Press, 2002), 187–207.

38 Veloso, Tropical, op cit. 311.

39 Veloso, Tropical, op cit. 306.

40 Veloso, Tropical, op cit. 309.

41 Veloso, Tropical, op cit. 309.

42 In 1993, Caetano published a vituperative response in the *Folha de São Paulo* ("Vá ver o 'Ham-Let' do Teatro Oficina") to a *New York Times* article by James Brooke which asserted that "Caetano Veloso and Gilberto Gil, two of Brazil's most famous singers, openly flaunt their bisexuality and wear dresses in public." http://www.nytimes.com/1993/08/12/world/rio-journal-in-live-and-let-live-land-gay-people-are-slain.html (accessed 19 March 2017). Brooke made this claim in the context of pondering the "paradox" of homophobic violence in a country that seemed to embrace carnivalesque expressions of sexual inversion. Caetano responded that he never wore dresses nor did he ever publicly pronounce himself bisexual—but he specified that the misrepresentations were troubling, not in themselves, but because they evidenced a lack of journalistic care both for the artists and for their nation, playing up a sexual caricature in order to titillate a U.S. readership and give an impression of Brazilian "absurdity." This incident precisely points to the ways in which, for Caetano, questions of sexual representation are inextricable from those of national stereotype and exploitation. In the *Folha* piece, Caetano says that his friends in the U.S., as well as his oldest son, had advised him not to respond angrily, in part because of futility, but also because at least some of them (his son included) surmised that Brooke's intention was not to ridicule him and Gil, but rather to praise what Brooke perceived as their "advanced" and "liberated" questioning of sexual mores. Caetano acknowledged this possibility, but was still outraged by what he felt was the underlying motive of caricature—a trend in U.S. representations of Brazil, dating, as we've seen, back to Carmen Miranda. He defended his choice not to accept his own depiction as a caricature of carnivalesque sexual inversion, saying, "I don't lower my head to the neocons, nor to the politically correct." (*O Mundo não é chato*, 277). (I confess that the occasional moments of estrangement that I've had with Caetano's public pronouncements on politically charged topics such as homophobia or racism have come at moments when he invokes the notion of "political correctness," which, to me, is a misleading term. It was coined by self-ironizing leftists in this country, but was appropriated by the right as an accusation of the left's lack of self-irony—and openness to other perspectives. I say this, of course, as somebody whose origins are also in the U.S., and on the left. Which makes these moments of estrangement particularly odd, because they're the moments my national and political origins come back to me—whereas, as I've said, Caetano has so often been the one to unmoor my sense of national identity …)

43 Veloso, Tropical Truth, op cit. 308.

44 Another such a song is Caetano's own "Etc." (on *Estrangeiro*), which calls to a future, unseeable, unknown beloved:

"Come, secret person, come, I'm calling you …" When I was pregnant with my son, before I knew his sex, I used to sing him/her this song, very lovingly.

45 *I'm Trying to Reach You*, 45.

46 If it appears to be a stretch to include here a choreographic analysis, perhaps it will seem less so if I tell you that Pina Bausch and Caetano were, in fact, collaborators and friends—and in fact in Wim Wenders's documentary film, *Pina* (2011), Lutz Förster performs a similarly charming solo dance to Caetano's "Leãozinho." Caetano has declared himself in print, more than once, to have been "*apaixonado*," in love, with Bausch as an artist, and he chose an image of one of her choreographies for the cover of his collected essays and occasional writings (*O mundo não é chato*, 170, 261, cover).

47 I hope it's obvious that I'm referring to her public persona, and that I hold it, and her, in the highest regard. I. Love. Julie. London.

48 https://www.youtube.com/watch?v=8SnHp-r4j3o (accessed 19 March 2017).

49 Charles Bernstein, *Attack of the Difficult Poems* (University of Chicago Press, 2012), 138 n.9.

50 Donald Clarke, *Billie Holiday: Wishing on the Moon* (Da Capo Press, New York, 2002), 337.

51 Holiday puts an especially precipitous dip on the word "paradise"—which sounds simultaneously flirtatious and mocking—but also, maybe, like an acknowledgment of the truth of her precious, if denigrated, body. Of course, "a trip to paradise" rings in a particular way for someone from a "tropical paradise" like Brazil—and Caetano's singing of the phrase, while absent of Holiday's vocal quirk, has a similarly undecidable quality. It holds up a mirror to the fantasy of purchased bliss, but it's not entirely self-ironizing.

52 William Zinsser writes: "Sometimes … the bridge begins and we think: 'Hey, What's he *doing*?' How is he going to get back out of this one in eight bars? … [T]he champion, by common agreement, is Johnny Green's 'Body and Soul,' a bridge unlike any other. The first four bars are in the key that's a half-tone above the home key … the next four bars are a half-tone *below* the home key … and all the harmonic changes required to bring off this feat of acrobatics, including the safe landing on the final chord, are so logical as to seem foreordained" (43).

53 *Cinema Transcendental* (1979).

54 This, of course, might help explain some of Lorraine Leu's weird choices, mentioned above, of examples of his "love songs."

55 "Tem uma música estranha e usa muitas palavras em *a*. Lembro que Augusto de Campos gostava muito dessa canção." The music is strange and the song uses a lot of words with the sound "*a*". I remember that Augusto de Campos really liked this song. (Sobre as letras, 31).

56 Nothing serves as a ground where my tears fall.

57 On the complicated history of the song, see Todd Decker, *Who Should Sing "Ol' Man River"?: The Lives of an American Song* (Oxford University Press, New York, 2014).

58 Her husband, Jack Webb, was the producer who'd first

commissioned Hamilton, at London's suggestion. See Michael Whorf, *American Popular Song Composers: Oral Histories, 1920s–1950s* (McFarland, Jefferson, NC, 2012, 91–6).

59   "A Small Voice Makes Big Stir," *Life*, February 18, 1957, 75.

60   This is the kind of thing I sometimes call a "Performance Studies $64,000 Question": the way in which the explicitness of performance can seemingly get closer to an affective "truth".

61   On the raced and gendered history of songs of disappointed love, see Ted Gioia, *Love Songs: The Hidden History* (Oxford University Press, New York, 2015). On the possible feminist recuperation of what might be perceived as the genre's depiction of women's victimization, see Stacy Holman Jones, *Torch Singing: Performing Resistance and Desire from Billie Holiday to Edith Piaf* (AltaMira Press, Lanham, MD, 2007)—and for a reading more specifically oriented around black feminism, see Angela Davis, *Blues Legacies and Black Feminism: Gertrude "Ma" Rainey, Bessie Smith, and Billie Holiday* (Vintage, New York, 1999).

62   A brief catalogue of some of the more varied ones: Joni Mitchell, *Blue*, 1971; Willie Nelson *Phases and Stages*, 1974; Bob Dylan, *Blood on the Tracks*, 1975; Marvin Gaye, *Here, My Dear*, 1978; Paul Simon, *Hearts and Bones*, 1983; Bruce Springsteen, *Tunnel of Love*, 1987; Alanis Morissette, *Jagged Little Pill*, 1995; Beck, *Guess I'm Doing Fine*, 2002; Justin Timberlake, *Justified*, 2004 (his "Cry Me a River"—about his break-up with Britney Spears—is distinct from Hamilton's—but clearly references the original as the epitome of the genre); Kanye West, *808s and Heartbreak*,

2007; Bon Iver, *For Emma, Forever Ago*, 2008; and Nas, *Life is Good*, 2012.

63 "Slavery will remain for a long time as the national characteristic of Brazil."

64 Gershwin, George, "Gershwin explains why his *Porgy and Bess* is called "'folk opera."' *New York Times* (November 2, 1935). For an analysis of Gershwin's actual debt to African-American music, see Jeffrey Melnick, *A Right to Sing the Blues: Jews, African Americans, and American Popular Song* (Harvard University Press, Cambridge, MA, 1999).

65 Ellen Noonan, *The Strange Career of Porgy and Bess: Race, Culture, and America's Most Famous Opera* (University of North Carolina Press, Chapel Hill, NC, 2012), 1, 3.

66 James Baldwin, *The Price of the Ticket: Collected Nonfiction, 1948–1985* (St. Martin's Press, New York, 1985) 180.

67 This strange and wonderful website documents many of the covers: http://www.summertime-connection.nl/ (accessed 19 March 2017).

68 "An Orpheus, Rising From Caricature" (*New York Times*, August 20, 2000).

69 Barack Obama's account, in his memoir, of his mother's adoration of Camus's film suggests something similar, though without the derisiveness (he is, after all, talking about his mother) of Baldwin and Caetano: "I suddenly realized that the depiction of the childlike blacks I was now seeing on the screen, the reverse image of Conrad's dark savages, was what my mother had carried with her … a reflection of the simple fantasies that had been forbidden to a white, middle-class girl from Kansas, the promise of another life: warm, sensual, exotic, different." Barack Obama, *Dreams from My Father: A Story of Race and Inheritance* (Times Books, New York, 1995, 124.)

70   Gilberto Freyre, *The Masters and the Slaves: A Study in the Development of Brazilian Civilization*, tr. Samuel Putnam (Random House, 1964).

71   Caetano also embraced a more recent work, *A Utopia brasileira e os movimentos negros*, by his longtime friend Antonio Risério (Editora 34, 2007), which also proposes, "outside the politically correct" position, a particularly hopeful configuration of racial admixture owing much to Freyre's. As I noted above (see note 42, above), such moments of disparagement of so-called "political correctness" tend to make me, ironically, feel my own national and political origins rear their—ugly? beautiful?— heads, even as I am sympathetic to the resistance to the kind of U.S.-splaining (I mean for this neologism, of course, to resonate with the, ahem, PC notion of "mansplaining": https://en.wikipedia.org/wiki/Mansplaining (accessed 19 March 2017)) that Caetano identifies in the work of many "Brazilianists"—a category into which I've sometimes been placed. Certainly, racism is a shamefully persistent problem in both countries, and it expresses itself very differently in each. On this, I think we can agree.

72   "A escravidão permanecerá por muito tempo como a característica nacional do Brasil … seu contato foi a primeira forma que recebeu a natureza virgem do país … insuflou-lhe sua alma infantile, suas tristezas sem pesar, suas lágrimas sem amargor, seu silêncio sem concentração, suas alegrias sem causa, sua felicidade sem dia seguinte …"

73   http://www.nonesuch.com/albums/noites-do-norte
(accessed 19 March 2017).

74   See, for example, Joe Tangari's review on Pitchfork, which
begins with a lament of U.S. ignorance of the specificities
of slave history in the rest of the Americas: http://pitchfork.
com/reviews/albums/8427-noites-do-norte/ (accessed 19
March 2017). See also Fernando Gonzalez, "From Brazil, A
Musician's Colorful Call," *Washington Post*, April 22, 2001: "In
'Noites do Norte' ('Northern Nights'), Caetano Veloso's style
ranges from samba to hip-hop to bossa nova to drum 'n'
bass to—believe it or not—classical music and noise rock.
A 19th-century abolitionist's words helped shape singer-
songwriter Caetano Veloso's new CD."

75   "[Brazil's] international reputation consists in slaveryesque
formulae such as the consummately festive spirit of its
people, the sexual availability of its 'racially mixed' women,
and the physical prowess of its athletes … An example
of the prevalence of this discourse is Caetano Veloso's
recent CD, 'Noites do Norte' (2000), wherein he invokes
the invariably heroicized abolitionist Joaquim Nabuco …"
Alexandra Isfahani-Hammond, *The Masters and the Slaves:
Plantation Relations and Mestizaje in American Imaginaries*
(Palgrave Macmillan, New York, 2007), 8.

76   Mapplethorpe's images were famously analyzed by Kobena
Mercer as racially fetishistic in a 1986 essay, "Imaging
the Black Man's Sex," though he revised his position in
a 1989 reconsideration of the question, "Skin Head Sex
Thing: Racial Difference and the Homoerotic Imagination,"
in which he suggested that perhaps it wasn't really so
clear whether Mapplethorpe was confirming or in fact

critiquing racist iconography. Mercer ultimately chose to hold both readings side by side. His original thesis and his subsequent revision of it both appear in his "Reading Racial Fetishism: The Photographs of Robert Mapplethorpe," in *Welcome to the Jungle: New Positions in Black Cultural Studies* (Routledge, New York, 1994), 171–220.

77 Tom Moon, "Returning to Brazil in samba, hip-hop," *Philadelphia Inquirer*, April 29, 2001. http://articles.philly.com/2001-04-29/entertainment/25331641_1_noites-tropicalia-movement-bossa (accessed 19 March 2017).

78 This is clearly an album in which track order is important to consider. See Introduction, note 53.

79 Of course, it might be argued that such a thing doesn't exist: some would define samba by its typically 2/4 time signature. But the song, which is an enchantment, carries the *feel* of a samba with an imposed trip-step, a tricky little hesitation which calls you dance to it even as it baffles your efforts. The track is beautifully arranged by Moreno Veloso, who plays the traditional, casual, domestic samba instrumentation of a plate and knife, as well as conga, pandeiro, bumbo, surdo, hand-clapping, and electric guitar—alongside other musicians, friends and family.

80 http://www.nonesuch.com/albums/noites-do-norte (accessed 19 March 2017).

81 "Haiti is here. Haiti is not here."

82 Geoffrey Holder, "That Fad from Trinidad," *New York Times*, April 21, 1957, 14.

83 The larger argument bears unpacking: see Shane Vogel,

"*Jamaica* on Broadway: The Popular Caribbean and Mock Transnational Performance," *Theatre Journal* 62 (2010): 1–21.

84 See note 7, above.

85 Gerard Béhague, "Rap, Reggae, Rock, or Samba: The Local and the Global in Brazilian Popular Music (1985–95)," *Latin American Music Review* 27 (1) (2006, 79–90): 84.

86 In the context of talking about the incorporation of diasporic forms into the Brazilian sound, it's important to note that Gil himself was a major proponent of reggae, covering Bob Marley in Portuguese, and touring with Jimmy Cliff. Christopher Dunn writes that Gil's "ongoing forays into reggae music contributed decisively to the expansion and indigenization of reggae throughout Brazil in the 1980s and 1990s." *Brutality Garden*, 185.

87 *Infectious Rhythm: Metaphors of Contagion and the Spread of African Culture* (Routledge, New York, 1998).

88 Ibid. 3–4.

89 I've already addressed some of the ways Ipanema has been configured in that iconography. Hawaii has its own place in the imaginary of popular music, notably in the music of the Beach Boys and of course Elvis Presley, whom I discuss below.

90 The reasons for this are complex, but surely stem from the fact that it was the site of the largest and most successful slave revolt in history. I discussed this in *Infectious Rhythm*, but for a fuller account, see Paul Farmer, *The Uses of Haiti* (Common Courage Press, Monroe, ME, 1994).

91 "Blue sky which comes down to where our feet touch the earth."

92 "Come meet life. I say, it's delicious."

93 On Brown, see note 7, above.

94 Brown's aesthetic, generally, might usefully be linked to the larger, diasporic notion of Afrofuturism. See Alondra Nelson, "Introduction: Future Texts," *Social Text* 20 (2) (2002): 1–15.

95 "It really didn't take a trained ear to appreciate that the Berlin contribution, "Blue Skies," was a great piece of songwriting, easily superior to anything Larry and I had written for the production." Richard Rodgers, *Musical Stages: An Autobiography* (Da Capo Press, New York, 2009), 96.

96 Andrea Most's *Making Americans: Jews and the Broadway Musical* (Harvard University Press, Cambridge, MA, 2004) offers a narrative in which Jewish songwriters and performers established a specific cultural (as opposed to racial) place in the formation of U.S. identity, in part through their appropriations of black culture. Michael Rogin's *Blackface, White Noise: Jewish Immigrants in the Hollywood Melting Pot* (University of California Press, Oakland, CA, 1996) similarly argues that, in the early twentieth century, Jewish performers employed blackface in an effort to assume white—that is, fully "American"—identity. In reference to *The Jazz Singer* in particular, Arthur Knight's *Disintegrating the Musical: Black Performance and American Musical Film* (Duke University Press, Durham, NC, 2002) follows Eric Lott's seminal work on blackface (*Love and Theft: Blackface Minstrelsy and the American Working*

Class [Oxford University Press, New York, 1993]) in reading the film as a simultaneous expression of love for and appalling parody of black culture, which "works to manage white anxieties about race" (57).

97 The seminal text on the blues as a genre of music wherein African-Americans enacted a critique of—and a critical intervention upon—U.S. national identity is Leroi Jones's (Amiri Baraka's) *Blues People: Negro Music in White America* (William Morrow, 1963). I've already mentioned Angela Davis's book turning the analysis of the genre toward gender and sexual politics. But the larger bibliography on the social significance of the blues is immense.

98 *A Arte Maior de Caetano Veloso* (1982), and *Caetano Veloso* (1986). In the first, after that opening phrase, he's joined by a chamber orchestra, while in the second the arrangement is limited to voice and guitar.

99 The definitive account of the origins of samba and its transformation into the "national" musical genre is Hermano Vianna's *Samba: Popular Music and National Identity in Brazil*, tr. John Charles Chasteen (University of North Carolina Press, Chapel Hill, NC, 1999). Vianna begins his account with the historic encounter of Gilberto Freyre (see above, p. 84) with a group of black and white artists and intellectuals from both elite and popular backgrounds. The fateful encounter, in Vianna's account, opened out into the collaborative "invention of tradition" that allowed for a narrative of racial and cultural mixity in musical form that would lead to an ensconcing of samba as an expression of hybrid national identity. Among them was the black sambista Donga, widely credited (though

Vianna says the song was a collective composition) as the author of the first recorded samba, "Pelo Telefone," with its refrain, "*Ai ai ai, é deixar mágoas pra trás, ó rapaz …*" Ai ai ai, the thing is to leave your wounds behind, young man …

100 Max Wilk, *The Making of* The Sound of Music (Routledge, 2007), 78.

101 There's also electric bass, and Caetano's guitar; Mônica Millet plays pandeiro, Naná Vasconcelos is credited on talking drum, *cerâmica*, and congas on the track—but the principal percussive sound is a plate and knife wielded by Dona Edith do Prato, a seventy-five-year-old public fixture from Caetano's home town. She also played on *Araçá Azul*.

102 So, of course, is the von Trapp family in *The Sound of Music*, even if the notion has to be sanitized through a narrative of widowerhood and the intention of religious celibacy.

103 Perhaps unsurprisingly, his younger sons are also musical. Zeca co-wrote a song ("Você me deu") with his father on Gal Costa's recent album (*Gal Estrátosférica* [Sony, 2015]), and Tom is the principal composer for the band Dônica (*Continuidades dos Parques* [Sony, 2015]).

104 Lest I give the impression that Moreno is exclusively interested in this genre of music, I should note that his range of musical interests extends much further, as is clear on his own recordings (see below). Like his father, he's interested in forms that range from the "folkloric" to classical, pop, experimental, and beyond. Caetano's recent swerve in sound was clearly inflected by musicians of his generation and circle—in fact, the Banda Cê is composed of them.

105 Moreno + 2, *Máquina de escrever* (RockIt!, 2001), Domenico + 2, *Sincerely Hot* (Luaka Bop, 2003), Kassin + 2, *Futurismo* (Luaka Bop, 2007) [of these albums, he is the composer on the first and collaborator on the second and third, in a project which serially shifted leadership of the + 2 band between its three members], and Moreno Veloso, *Coisa Boa* (Disco Maravilha, 2014).

106 Will Friedwald, *Sinatra! The Song is You: A Singer's Art* (Da Capo Press, New York, 1997), 166.

107 https://twitter.com/ladygaga/status/511747807330312192 (accessed 19 March 2017).

108 *Tropical Truth*, 10.

109 Sá is a highly original and exploratory musician, a contemporary and collaborator of Moreno's, who is part of the Banda Cê that backs Caetano on his recent trio of recordings, which were co-produced by Sá and Moreno.

110 http://www.shadowboxstudio.com/ahbefiles/correction. html (accessed 19 March 2017).

111 When I read about ahbez's dissatisfaction with the song, I tried singing it in my head like that, with the amended ending, the way he would have wanted it. I imagined he might have left that final, repeated phrase, "just to love and be loved," hanging in the air, repeating the suspended notes, without resolving the melody on a closing tonic. I liked it better that way, suspended, unresolved. Still open.

Rock and Pop

Diana

Hold me, darling, ho-ho hold me tight,
Squeeze me baby with a-all your might.
PAUL ANKA, "DIANA"

Baby, baby, I love you.
CAETANO VELOSO, "BABY"

"Diana" was written and recorded by Paul Anka when he was still a teenager, and it shot him to fame. Anka was born and raised in Ontario, Canada, and though he became a naturalized U.S. citizen some years later, he was Canadian when he wrote the song, meaning it's an "American" song only in the broad sense of the term. But it was part of the massive, inundating tide of exuberant rock that was flooding far beyond national borders in the late '50s. And it was also taking other American sounds in. As Reebee Garofalo writes, from the outset of rock's history, "countless" songs have "appropriated Latin rhythms, some with more success and credibility than others." Garofalo's first example is "teen idol" Paul Anka's "Diana."[1] The song was released in 1957, which you'll remember was the year of the calypso craze. Anka's song was one of a number of songs that attempted to merge Caribbean rhythms into rock, giving rise to a dance fad, popularized on Dick Clark's *American Bandstand*, called "chalypso." It was ostensibly a mix of the cha-cha-cha (itself a bastardization of the mambo) and calypso. Needless to say, there was a lot of imagining of "Latin" movement—and sound—going on.

For Caetano, who was also a teenager when the song came out, "Diana" was part of that wash of English-language music that was exasperatingly compelling copycat performances by young Brazilians. For those whose mastery of English was limited, there were a few signal words to grab onto. Maybe the most important was: baby. A decade later, Caetano and his *tropicalista* conspirators released *Tropicália, ou Panis et Circensis*, the manifesto album of the movement. The first song on the B side was the album's hit single: "Baby." Caetano composed it, and Gal Costa[2] sang it, Caetano joining in at the very end to interlace her lines, "Baby, baby, I love you," with a fragment of Anka's song, "Diana …"

"Baby" is, in Christopher Dunn's words, "an exquisite pop song."[3] Indeed, maybe a perfect song. Yes, I'll go ahead and say it, it's a perfect song. It's a catalogue of various things that the narrator tells "you" you need to have, or do, or know: an upscale swimming pool, an artificial butter product, a song by Roberto Carlos, gas for the car, ice cream at a diner, the English language … and especially the words printed on his t-shirt: "Baby, baby, I love you." Gal sings it beautifully, in a languid, open tone, and it's hard to tell if you're meant to be mortified or entirely seduced by the list of bourgeois comforts and "American" influences. The song itself is both a critique of and a loving hommage to pop music. It *is* pop music.

Caetano's version of "Diana" on *A Foreign Sound*, like "Baby," is supported by strings, with a subtle but insistent 6/8 rhythm behind it. And, at the very end,[4] he inserts a fragment of … his own song: "Baby, baby, I love you … Diana …" It's another double-edged love song, this one not just to "America" and to her music, but also to his own exquisite, ambivalent song.

Love Me Tender

Love me tender, love me true, all my dreams fulfill.
KEN DARBY AND GEORGE R. POULTON (CREDITED TO ELVIS PRESLEY AND VERA MATSON), "LOVE ME TENDER"

"You're not allowed in here, get out."
That's what rock 'n' roll is all about.
CAETANO VELOSO, "NOSTALGIA"[5]

Remember those horrible things that Frank Sinatra said about rock 'n' roll? The context was a 1957 article in the French press in which he spoke about the new musical form sweeping the nation. Sinatra didn't single out any particular "cretin" as responsible for the apparent collapse not just of his nation's popular music but, it would appear, Western civilization. But a lot of people seemed to think he was referencing a particular person: Elvis Presley. The *Herald-Express* asked Elvis for a response. It was measured: "I admire the man," he said. "He has a right to his own opinions. He is a great success and a fine actor, but I don't think he should have said it. I don't think anyone has the right to take potshots at something that is definitely a trend. It's an American development, just like crooning was a few years back."[6] Sinatra himself acknowledged that, when he was starting out, people similarly regarded him as something of a "freak." He said time would tell if Elvis had what it took to last.

Shortly after that little brouhaha, Elvis was drafted into the military. When he was honorably discharged in 1960, Sinatra invited him to appear on his television special, the "Frank Sinatra Timex Show." Evidently, they both considered it an opportunity to expand their audiences. At the end of the program, they sang a duet, alternating bits of each other's songs. Elvis sang lines from Frank's standard, "Witchcraft." Frank sang lines from "Love Me Tender." It's a weird performance, simultaneously both parody of and hommage to one another. Frank's "Love Me Tender" is upbeat, finger-snapping, and swinging. But when they get to the final line, they harmonize, slowly and sweetly, and Frank pauses, his arm around Elvis, to say, "Man, that's pretty!" It is, but there's a tiny hint that calling Elvis's music "pretty" might be a mild dig at Presley's masculinity. Yet both singers had done something to reconfigure what "manliness" in popular song meant. I already mentioned that Sinatra's torch songs staked a masculine claim on the possibility of expressing heartache. Presley's stage persona has often been spoken about in relation to racial inflections,[7] but his controversial pelvic grinds were also unsettling because they seemed to draw on female erotic performance. And then there was tenderness.[8]

"Love Me Tender" was written over the melody of the Civil War-era "Aura Lee" by George Putnam. Ken Darby wrote a new lyric for Presley to sing in his film debut, and the song gave the film its title. While other songs in the film gave Elvis a chance to shake, rattle and roll (weirdly, since the story is itself set in the Civil War era), the tender ballad was strategic not only in making his character sympathetic, but also in presenting another side to Presley's persona. It was a massive hit. It could have been written for a crooner—and in fact Nat King Cole performed it on his TV show in the '50s. So did the Lennon Sisters. Percy Sledge recorded it in the '60s, as did BB King in the '80s. But it's pretty indelibly linked to the historical moment when a rocker and a crooner collided, trying to figure out where U.S. popular music was going.

That confusing torrent of sounds—Sinatra and Elvis, Nat King Cole and Louis Armstrong, cool jazz—as well as Mexican, Cuban, Argentinian, and of course national music—was washing over Brazil as well, and as a teenager Caetano was trying to figure out how to navigate all that. His memoir notes, in particular, his youthful disinterest in Elvis, with his "heavy, masculine vibrato." It was only subsequently, through a kind of Warholian insight, that he'd develop an interest in Elvis as a sign of "the unprecedented force of mass media"[9]—a question that would become central to the *tropicalistas*. But in the late '50s, musically, for him, it was bossa nova that was the astonishment. Caetano cites a 1988 *Village Voice* review of a concert by João Gilberto in which Julian Dibbell called João "Brazil's Elvis." Caetano duly notes that Dibbell was sort of joking, but he finds the analogy interesting, "for what it makes conspicuous above all are the nearly diametrical origins of bossa nova and rock: bossa nova's revival of samba evolved from a refinement of musical tastes that was influenced by high-quality American songs of the thirties and by the cool jazz of the fifties; by contrast, rock in its essence was a rejection of all sophistication, and continually proves to be so whenever it seeks its own reaffirmation, as the wildly commercial and regressive style of music it was from the beginning."[10] For all that he initially rejected incipient rock and its mimicry in Brazil, its willful regression and "wild commercialism" would prove food for thought in the late '60s.

Caetano's version of "Love Me Tender" begins with Jaques Morelenbaum's delicate, toy-like celesta. Caetano's voice enters in his upper range, in the key of C (Elvis sings it nearly an octave below, in D). In fact, when I listened to it side by side with "Cucurrucucú Paloma," I realized they're in the same key, with the lines "love me tender, love me true, all my dreams fulfill" hitting precisely the notes of the "cucurrucucú …" You could almost superimpose one on the other (in fact, I tried this, and it was surprisingly beautiful). If Elvis used the song to ostensibly let the public glimpse, for a moment, his tender part, Caetano takes that tenderness, literally, to a higher level.

It's Alright Ma (I'm Only Bleeding)

Who despise their jobs, their destinies,
Speak jealously of them that are free …
BOB DYLAN, "IT'S ALRIGHT MA (I'M ONLY BLEEDING)"

Eles tomam bonde no dia de amanhã
Eles amam os filhos no dia de amanhã.[11]
CAETANO VELOSO, "ELES"

Caetano says in his memoir that, when he first heard Dylan, he was intrigued by his droning, nasal voice and his raw musicianship, but that the words were somewhat incomprehensible to him so he ended up bored. But once the *tropicália* movement was in full swing, he went back to listening to Dylan and became fascinated, in particular, with *Bringing It All Back Home*. That, of course, is the album that contains "It's Alright Ma," which Caetano covers on *A Foreign Sound*. *Bringing It All Back Home* has an acoustic side and an electric side, and it was released just months before the cataclysmic performance that Elijah Wald has called "the night that split the '60s."[12] On July 25, 1965, Dylan mounted the stage at the Newport Folk Festival, plugged into an amp, and howled his independence from folk orthodoxy. The response from the crowd is the stuff of legend: a cacophony of outrage mixed with possible strains of ecstasy. If the encounter between a crooner and a rocker had been awkward, that between folk and electric was pure combustion.

Three years later, on September 15, 1968, at the *Festival Internacional de Canção* in Rio, there was a similar—some would say parallel—combustion. Backed by the São Paulo psychedelic rockers Os Mutantes, Caetano took to the stage to perform his song "É proibido proibir"—"It's forbidden to forbid"—a slogan taken from the May '68 uprising in France. Ironically, the leftist student activists in the audience seemed to want to do just that—to foreclose the performance with a hailstorm of boos. The reaction had everything to do with a rejection of electric rock, which they considered an importation of the imperialist sounds from the north. Caetano had intended to be provocative—three days earlier at the festival, he'd already encountered the crowd's resistance, which just got worse when he was joined on stage by a U.S. "hippie" rocker friend, John Danduran, whose assigned role was basically to shriek. Gilberto Gil had similarly been rejected at the festival for a Hendrix-inflected performance of his "Questão de Ordem" (Question of Order).[13] But when things came to a head on September 15, Caetano let it rip. A large part of the audience had turned its back on the performers, who retaliated by doing the same. The outraged students who still faced the stage pelted it with fruit and eggs. Gil came on stage to lend his support, and Caetano launched into a diatribe. His fury that day is also the stuff of legend: "But what kind of youth is this? ... You know who you guys are equal to? Is there sound in the mic? Do you know who you're equal to?" He told the students that they were no different from the very censorious right that they ostensibly opposed, including the military police who had just brutally shut down a left-leaning theatrical production. "You're not different from them at all. You're not at all different ... The problem is, you're trying to police Brazilian music! ... But Gil and I have opened the path, and what is it you want? I came here to put an end to all of this. Gilberto Gil is here with me to put an end to the Festival and all this imbecility that reigns in Brazil. No one's ever heard me talk like this before, you understand? And I just want to say this, baby, if you are the same in politics as you are in aesthetics, we're done for."[14]

Pedro Alexandre Sanches has noted that both Dylan's and Caetano's conflagrations with their publics over going electric didn't, ultimately, erode their positions as icons of their respective national musics. On the contrary. And both have continued, throughout their careers, to shape-shift unapologetically—in fact, with a vengeance.[15] Given those two seemingly parallel stories, perhaps it's not surprising that some of the thematic preoccupations of their songs in that period should overlap. Both artists were bent on critiquing the violent and stifling politics of the right, but they were equally suspicious of a self-congratulatory and sometimes narrow-minded left. That's the sting in many of the songs on *Bringing It All Back Home*. Caetano's *tropicália*-period lyrics also agonize over complacency, hypocrisy, and fear of the future. And some of Dylan's rebukes have continued to resonate in Caetano's lyrics, even in later compositions. "O Estrangeiro," for example, has a passage about the emperor who has no clothes—a passage that seems to echo Dylan's observation in "It's Alright Ma" that "even the president of the United States" sometimes has to be naked.

So why is it that of all the songs on *A Foreign Sound*, this is the track that sounds the most foreign in Caetano's mouth, the very song from which the album takes its name? John Bush's review on allmusic.com gives the album 4½ out of 5 stars, and fairly gushes over nearly every track, except for this: "Out of 22 songs, only Bob Dylan's 'It's Alright, Ma (I'm Only Bleeding)' sounds like a mistake."[16] But whereas Bush seems to find the strangeness of the track to be a flaw, I find it, actually, trenchant, poignant, necessary. That sound is, precisely, a foreign sound— but also one of recognition, even if, here, it's difficult to identify who is Odysseus, and who the swineherd Eumaeus.[17]

The arrangement of "It's Alright Ma" on *A Foreign Sound* is a layering of electric guitar, *mangue beat*[18] drums, hip-hop scratches, and programed percussion—that is, it's an eclectic but supremely contemporary mix of instrumental sounds that have already been through the blender of U.S./Brazilian musical relations. Caetano's vocal appears to be an attempt to approximate Dylan's longwinded nasal drone. It's a fucking long lyric. There's a reason there aren't many covers.[19] It sounds weird. But for all that he seems to be, in that vocal, attempting to *recognize* Dylan, there's also a way in which Caetano's version of this song seems to insist steadfastly on his own foreignness in relation to it. The track ends (apparently opaquely for some U.S. listeners) with a brief snatch from a song from the soundtrack of Glauber Rocha's film, *Deus e o Diabo na Terra do Sol*: "'*Se entrega, Corisco!' 'Eu não me entrego, não.*'"[20] Corisco is a backlands outlaw in the film. The line demands: "Give yourself up, Corisco!" and he answers, "I'm not giving myself up, no."

At least one Brazilian critic noted that significant insertion when Caetano appeared at Carnegie Hall upon the release of *A Foreign Sound*: "One might ask if the show … in which Caetano declared his identification with America—the whole continent [*sic*], including the United States—might not orient our reading [of the album]. Like in the insertion, at the end of 'It's Alright Ma (I'm Only Bleeding),' by Bob Dylan, of the verses … 'Give yourself up, Corisco! I'm not giving myself up, no.' But no, because that was already there, in the verses of 'Love for Sale,' by Cole Porter: 'Who's prepared to pay the price / for a trip to paradise?'"[21] Nice connection. And it makes you ask another question: which is the paradise, Brazil, or the U.S.? And, precisely, who is willing to pay what price?

If It's Magic

If it's magic,
Why can't we make it everlasting?
STEVIE WONDER, "IF IT'S MAGIC"

In 1977, the FESTAC black arts festival was held in Nigeria. Fela Kuti had argued with the festival organizers and refused to perform in it, but a number of visiting international artists attended an alternative event at his Afrika Shrine. Among them were Gilberto Gil and Stevie Wonder. Caetano missed the activities at the Shrine, though he attended all the FESTAC events with Gil. That trip, and the musical encounters it occasioned, were important to Caetano, though probably even more so for Gil. If Caetano has been occasionally dubbed "the Bob Dylan of Brazil," among U.S. artists Gil is most frequently compared to Stevie Wonder.[22] In fact, they've recorded and performed together (notably at a massive outdoor concert on Copacabana in 2012), and Gil has covered some of Wonder's songs, including "The Secret Life of Plants," and a Portuguese version he made of "I Just Called to Say I Love You." Stevie Wonder has a peculiar knack for writing seemingly inevitable, undeniably permanent pop songs. Of course, his opus has some challenging and very original songs as well—among them "The Secret Life of Plants."[23] And while Gil may appear to be the one with a more pop-oriented sound in the line of Stevie Wonder, Caetano has also written a number of songs that have that same feel of inevitability—songs with an overwhelming mass appeal. Their sound is not always so very far from Wonder's—in fact, if you try interspersing the verses and the refrains of "Você é linda" and "I Just Called to Say I Love You," the mesh is seamless.

Caetano's cover of "If It's Magic" counterintuitively moves, again, in the direction of the young Brazilian experimentalists he's worked with, or that Moreno's worked with, in recent years. The track is arranged by Pedro Sá, along with Kassin, who has recorded with Moreno as a member of +2, and Berna Ceppas, who plays in another of Moreno's ensembles, the Orquestra Imperial. Pedro's highly distorted, wobbly, watery electric guitar chords form most of the backdrop, with some sparse beats. Some eerie electronic sounds— buzzes, clicks, and rattles—begin to infiltrate the tissue of the song, but largely there's empty space, the canvas for Caetano's vocal, which is precise, undramatic, but sustained, with a tight vibrato. The interpretation's modernity contrasts starkly with Wonder's: he's accompanied exclusively by a harp (!), until the closing stanzas, when his harmonica enters to leaven things. The apparent chiasmus in Caetano's version between Wonder's sweetness and an acerbic instrumental style puts pressure on the question of pop's encounter with the "aesthetes" of edge.

Detached

I don't have too much detachment.
I just get in there and I play scrabble.
DNA, "DETACHED"

Ela é tão jovem,
E tem saudade do tempo em que muita gente tinha
isqueiro.[24]
CAETANO VELOSO AND ARTO LINDSAY, "ELA ELA"

If Dylan's electric guitar felt like an affront to folk musicians, there would be others who would take the notion of instrumental "noise"—and edge—to an extreme degree. The seminal no wave band DNA—fetishized by die-hard fans, influential in various art scenes, but still configured as part of a short-lived underground movement—was formed in 1978 by Arto Lindsay (vocals and noise guitar) and Robin Crutchfield (keyboards). They recruited Ikue Mori, utterly inexperienced at the time, to play drums. Later Tim Wright would replace Crutchfield on bass. DNA dissolved in 1982. The no wave movement that Arto helped found in the '70s embraced difficult sounds, taking on aspects of a punk aesthetic, but also arty minimalism. Simon Reynolds describes DNA's signature sound: "'Skeletal, stop-start, lots of silences,' as Arto Lindsay put it, the songs often seemed to disassemble themselves in front of your ears … Lindsay's 'singing' consisted of animalistic barks and growls, flubbed vocal smears and shamanic grunts."[25] That's something of a cartoon version of the vocals—Arto himself has said that what he hears in those early recordings is an "untutored blues" voice, and it's interesting to listen to them that way. In later work, he'd adopt a vocal style bearing a stronger resemblance to Chet Baker or João Gilberto than to a "shamanic grunt." In fact, though he's maintained his idiosyncratic "non-musical" guitar technique, he's an extraordinarily musical person. But if you listen to the original recording of "Detached,"[26] you'll hear some guttural sounds.

Arto would go on to play in other bands (including Ambitious Lovers, which he formed with Peter Scherer) and on his own,[27] but also to collaborate with and produce a number of artists, many of them Brazilian—among them, and perhaps most significantly, Caetano. They became not only collaborators, but also close friends. Though born in the U.S., Arto spent much of his childhood and adolescence in Brazil, and he was profoundly impacted by his contact with the *tropicália* movement. Caetano describes their meeting in his memoir:

> When I went [to New York] for my record label … I met an obvious American waiting for me at JFK Airport. I tried to speak English to him, but he answered me in a perfectly Pernambucan Portuguese: it was Arto Lindsay, an atonal guitarist and historic figure in the music scene of the southern part of the island of Manhattan … A friendship was born.[28]

So was a collaborative relationship. Arto would go on to produce two of Caetano's most highly regarded albums, *Estrangeiro* in 1989 and *Circuladô* in 1991. There's a track on the latter album, "Ela Ela," ("Her Her") composed by the two of them, in which Arto plays his skronky guitar, leaving wide gaps of unnerving silence, as Caetano sings delicately, alternating between his low and high ranges, about "her" (presumably Paula Lavigne), with whom he attended a concert by Sting at Madison Square Garden, where she lamented the fact that nobody lit up cigarette lighters any more at concerts because everybody (herself included) had quit smoking. Cigarettes, Caetano observes in a suddenly assertive speaking voice, were invented by indigenous South Americans. It's a momentary tropicalist insertion into an hommage to a downtown New York radical art scene that in fact had been influenced by tropicalism from the get-go.

Caetano's conversations with Arto have had an ongoing effect on his thinking about musical idioms. Arto began his musical career in that downtown art world, in which experimentation in visual, performance, and sonic art overlapped. He's continued to make work in all these realms.[29] In his music, he's explored atonality and dissonance, aligning himself with the classical avant-garde, but he's shown no disdain for popular forms, from samba to soul and beyond (he loves a good groove). In this respect, he's demonstrated an eclecticism similar to that of the *tropicalistas*, who drew from the art of the vanguard, while simultaneously, stead-fastly, attempting to make themselves available to a wider audience.

As I mentioned above, when I told Arto I was writing about *A Foreign Sound* he expressed enthusiasm, mentioning both the "overthinking" and the sheer beauty of the album, which cuts through all that. He said he was honored by Caetano's choice to perform a version of the DNA song: "hearing him sing 'i just get in there and i play scrabble' is pretty priceless." It is. It's also a little jarring—though the disjunction here seems a bit more obviously intentional than on "It's Alright Ma." "Detached" is the one other track, besides that one, in which Caetano appears to be stretching toward a vocal style truly foreign to his own. Whereas he sounds like himself on "Ela Ela," on the DNA cover he doesn't. As I've said, he's certainly experimented before with ostensibly "unmusical" sounds. *Araçá Azul* was perhaps as willfully challenging to listeners as DNA was. But the strained moan on this track almost doesn't seem to be coming from his own throat. Still, the dissonance is given a context—one that stretches beyond the downtown moment of no wave, toward a vaster lineage of challenging music. Morelenbaum (credited as both transcriber and conductor) has replicated the song's disjunctive instrumental noise in orchestral form. Arto's skronk guitar and Tim Wright's wildly arbitrary head-banging bass are meticulously transposed onto a string ensemble, with drummer Marcio Bahia painstakingly reproducing Ikue Mori's splattered rhythmic outbursts. The arrangement, of course, makes clear an affiliation with classical vanguardism. Caetano's voice is there to remind you of that other aspect of no wave, one that was both indebted to the *tropicalistas*, and also, well, foreign to them: punk mayhem.

(Nothing But) Flowers / Feelings

Years ago, I was an angry young man.
I'd pretend that I was a billboard …
DAVID BYRNE, "(NOTHING BUT) FLOWERS"

Feelings, nothing more than feelings …
MORRIS ALBERT, "FEELINGS"

The no wave and art rock scene where Arto got his start was also populated by some figures who would manage to torque some of those awkward sounds toward a wider audience. Perhaps the most conspicuous was David Byrne, whose band Talking Heads achieved not only critical but also commercial success. The band was never averse to popular appeal, nor to the pleasures of crowd-pleasing music. Simon Reynolds quotes Byrne as "dislik[ing] 'art rock' as a label because of its connotation of dispassionate dabbling, the implication being that Talking Heads didn't 'have sincere feelings about our music or we're just flirting with rock and roll and we're too reserved and detached to rock out onstage.'"[30] Throughout his career, Byrne has been open to pop stardom, though with some of the same analytical curiosity that has animated Caetano's path as a *cantor de rádio*. And also, like Caetano, Byrne was interested in using a pop platform to explore, in Reynolds's words, not just the typical preoccupations of rock (love, sex, and rebellion), but also, or instead, "the whole vast realm of other stuff that makes up the world (bureaucracy, TV, animals, appliances, cities)."

Dairy Queens. Shopping malls. "(Nothing But) Flowers" is one of the tracks on *Naked*, the 1988 album that Talking

Heads recorded in Paris shortly before the band dissolved. They took a new tack on the album, availing themselves of the cosmopolitan musicians based in Paris. On this track, Abdou M'Boup added percussion, including talking drum, and Yves N'Djock played infectious, repetitive electric guitar riffs, giving a buoyant, West African feel to the song—ironically, since the song is so specifically located in a U.S. landscape—or rather, a possibly utopian, possibly dystopian vision of that landscape obliterated. More than one listener has heard it as an ironic overturning of Joni Mitchell's "Big Yellow Taxi" in which "they paved paradise and put up a parking lot." This time, the familiar terrain of 7-Elevens and strip malls has gotten overgrown with fields of daisies. It's unsettling to the song's narrator.[31]

Was the song a prescient warning about global warming and the Anthropocene? Or was it an ironic jab at self-congratulatory environmentalism? Frankly, the groove is so irresistible you can go with either reading—or both. Byrne shares with Lindsay a penchant for some opacity in his lyrics. It's not for nothing that Jonathan Demme's 1984 concert film of Talking Heads was titled *Stop Making Sense*. Which certainly doesn't mean Byrne's songs are senseless, but they often leave some of the construction of meaning to the listener. But perhaps the even greater mystery in his music has to do with the question of affect, or *feelings*. Byrne himself has recently suggested a self-diagnosis of mild Asperger's syndrome[32]—which might explain a thing or two. Undecidable irony is one of Byrne's contributions to popular music. If Caetano recognized in Warhol a certain wordless awe before popular culture, David

Byrne brought some of that blank affect to U.S. popular song. Which is not to say that he doesn't care. He says in *How Music Works*, "I am moved by more music now than I have ever been."[33] It's clear he *has* feelings—it's just not always obvious what those feelings are.

In Caetano's memoir, he recalls meeting Byrne at a 1986 film festival in Rio in which they were both presenting their own films (Caetano's *Cinema Falado* and Byrne's *True Stories*). Byrne had been traveling in Brazil, and was filled with (in this case evident) enthusiasm for the music he'd been hearing. In '88, he would found his label, Luaka Bop, and begin releasing compilations of Brazilian music, exposing various styles to a large U.S. audience.[34] In this period, Byrne was profoundly impacted by his encounter not only with the emerging sounds of Brazil, but also with older popular music—including Caetano's. He also began listening, intensely, to the composers of bossa nova. "I realized that although many of their songs were rich, harmonically complex, and, yes, beautiful, they definitely weren't shallow … I began to realize that depth, radical visions, and beauty were not mutually exclusive."[35] Caetano's recordings were among those that moved him. And Caetano's cover of "(Nothing But) Flowers" seems determined to deliver some feeling back.

There's percussion on the arrangement, but it's less groove-driven than the original. The dominant guitars are acoustic, and the tempo's slower. Caetano's vocal expresses not one, but *both* of the possibilities I suggested above—that is, it seems to have moments of sincere bewilderment, and moments of high irony. The final lines fade out in a rainy patter of percussion, and then the faint strains of Satie's first Gymnopédie on a music box.

After that initial meeting in 1986, Caetano and Byrne's mutual admiration—and friendship—would grow. Not only did Caetano record a Talking Heads cover on *A Foreign Sound*. He also dedicated another track to Byrne: "Feelings," by Morris Albert. It's partly a love song to a friend who's placed himself somewhere on the very mild end of the autism spectrum. But it's a song that lies, unapologetically, in the dead center of pop. It's also a song that raises some interesting ironies (oh hello, undecidable irony) about where one locates the borders between Brazilian and U.S. popular song. The lyrics were written by Morris Albert in 1974 to the melody of a 1957 song, "Pour Toi," by the French songwriter Loulou Gasté.[36] Albert recorded it, and it was hugely popular. For many, the song would seem to be the epitome of a banal pop ballad: a song so determined to tug at one's heartstrings that the very question of sincerity seems a joke. A number of artists covered it, often in live performance, including Ella Fitzgerald, Sarah Vaughan, and perhaps most famously Nina Simone. What each of them was thinking when they performed it is difficult to say. Simone's version, at the 1976 Montreux Jazz Festival, is extremely disorienting. She seems to be performing the virtuosic technique of actually imbuing pop banality with all of the intense, genuine, raw emotion that the song simultaneously names and forecloses. It's so *felt* it's embarrassing. The audience seems entirely discomfited at the end. They're not even sure if they should clap.

She makes some alterations in the lyric. Almost all interpreters of the song do—because, in fact, the grammar is a little weird. To tell the truth, when I first heard Caetano's version, which leaves the lyric intact, I was confused—I thought he'd made a mistake, which was odd, because his English is excellent. But the error is Morris Albert's: "I wish I've never met you, girl." Why was his English flawed? Well, one explanation would be that Morris Albert was Brazilian. Maurício Alberto Kaisermann. He took on Morris Albert as his artistic name. In a 2004 interview, Albert said: "I composed and sang in English, my idols spoke English, they were our influence, and I spoke the language well, my grandparents were English. The funny thing is, to this day, there are people who think I'm American, even though from the beginning I insisted I was Brazilian ... I'm proud of my roots, singing in English didn't transform me into a foreigner."[37] "Feelings" was the biggest-selling Brazilian single of all times. Maybe that's why in the U.S., as Jaques Morelenbaum wryly observes in the liner notes of *A Foreign Sound*, nobody believes that "Feelings" is a Brazilian song. Morelenbaum gives it the full, swelling but dignified orchestral treatment. And Caetano handles the lyric with the most delicate touch, allowing the fervor to mount at points, but pulling back to a near whisper on the famous "whoa-oh-oh," which he renders, discreetly, "oh, oh, oh ... again in my arms ..." And the orchestra pulls out one last, fading, but dissonant, chord.

Come as You Are

Come as you are, as you were,
As I want you to be.

KURT COBAIN, "COME AS YOU ARE"

Despite that line about Nirvana being "rubbish," in the official video for Caetano's version of "Come as You Are" he's shown, documentary-style, walking toward the stage, saying: "Kurt Cobain, I think he was a wonderful composer, he sang the songs very well … revitalizer of rock 'n' roll … For this album that I recorded, 'Come as You Are' was the inevitable song." Then he performs it—gorgeously.

Cobain has been memorialized—embalmed—in the tragic story of a beautiful, sad, gifted, tortured young person who sacrificed himself on the altar of rock 'n' roll. I myself once wrote of him as "the Mayakovsky of his generation,"[38] which was and wasn't an ironic suggestion. Nirvana isn't, wasn't, rubbish, and Caetano was trying to be provocative when he said they were. Maybe Kurt Cobain wasn't Mayakovsky, but the tragedy of his life was that so many people wanted him to be that—and a rock star too.

Cobain himself kept insisting he was defective as an artist—a guitarist of minimal skills, a songwriter with a limited formula who tossed in the words at the end, not really sure what he meant to say, or if it mattered. But all that self-abnegation should probably be taken with a grain of salt. When Cobain came of age, musically, punk had already pushed the disavowal of skill in rock to its limit, but its vitality was a force of nature. Grunge also disavowed talent and technique—as well as any energetic drive that you could call Dionysian or truly anarchic. Ironically, in Cobain, the combination of a self-avowed lack of both skills and energy became the very thing other rockers aspired to: the new ideal. And his discomfort with rock star status just seemed to fuel the fascination, even as he seemed to want to kick it off.

Hugh Barker and Yuval Taylor open their book, *Faking It: The Quest for Authenticity in Popular Music*,[39] with Cobain as the grand exemplar of honesty in performance. They note Cobain's occasional self-mythologizing, and the fact that his disdain for "sell-out" bands was belied by his own ambition, but at the level of musical performance he approaches, in their reading, real nakedness—raw emotion laid bare. It's hard to construe Cobain's expressions of pain as anything but honest, given his end. But sometimes artifice, too, can be revealing—and compelling. In Nirvana's original version of "Come as You Are," the vocal, to my ear, has clearly affected qualities—that somewhat forced growl, a weird British accent on "*soaked* in bleach." Those moments move me *because of* their artifice, not in spite of it. It's not unrelated to what I said about Julie London's torch singing.

Still, I confess, though he himself would probably resist this: I'm even more compelled by Caetano's version of the song. Instrumentally, it's pared back. Pedro Sá's electric guitar and Moreno Veloso's cello have an unprocessed, almost plunky sound compared with Cobain's guitar's blurry wash effect. In the place of crashing drums, there's the spare finger tap of a *tamborim*. For Pedro and Moreno's generation of musicians, of course, Cobain occupied something like the place that Elvis occupied for Caetano at the outset of his career. Which doesn't mean that this generation of exploratory Brazilian musicians have looked to *emulate* U.S. indie rock, but they've had to reckon with it. And the sound that came out of that reckoning has inflected Caetano's recordings over the last decade with the Banda Cê.

Caetano's voice on this track is seemingly affectless—with a pure diction and a precise phrasing that inevitably draw your attention to the words of the song. Caetano has said that, when he came to New York for the release of *A Foreign Sound*, a chauffeur told him that he'd never really understood the words of "Come as You Are" until he heard Caetano's version. Of course, "understanding" those words is a complex proposition. In interviews, Cobain would often say he had no idea what he meant when he wrote the lyrics to his songs. His bandmate, Krist Novoselic, told *Rolling Stone* that Cobain liked to remain "cryptic." He also said, "He wanted to be a rock star— and he hated it."[40] Caetano's relationship to composition—and to being a rock star—is very different. He once told me that at first he was flummoxed by the indecipherable lyrics of a certain strain of U.S. rock—until he figured out that that was the point. But his interpretation of "Come as You Are" gives one a sense of a direct address to a friend, to an old enemy. It's an address of both intimacy and empathy. In fact, maybe that gentle "Come, take a rest" could be directed at Cobain himself. From one rock star to another.

Notes

1 Reebee Garofalo, "Off the Charts: Outrage and Exclusion in the Eruption of Rock and Roll," in Rachel Rubin and Jeffrey Paul Melnick, eds., *American Popular Music: New Approaches to the Twentieth Century* (University of Massachusetts Press, Amherst, MA, 2001), 122.

2 Gal has also been a lifelong collaborator of Caetano's. They recorded the album *Domingo* (Philips) together in 1967, and have often worked together since.

3 Christopher Dunn, *Brutality Garden*, 109.

4 In fact, the arrangement of "Diana" begins as well with a brief but clear melodic quotation from "Baby"—a detail that's immediately perceptible to listeners familiar with Caetano's discography. It's perhaps the most explicitly self-referential moment on the album, even as it points back to his own early pop influences.

5 On *Transa*.

6 Cited in Alan Hanson, "Did Sinatra Really Bad Mouth Elvis and His Music in '57?" www.elvis-history-blog.com (accessed 19 March 2017).

7 The bibliography on Elvis Presley's debt to black popular culture and its political ramifications is enormous. For a skeptical take, emphasizing the question of appropriation, see Maureen Mahon, *Right to Rock: The Black Rock Coalition and the Cultural Politics of Race* (Duke University Press, Durham, NC, 2004), which encapsulates much of the critique leveled by writers and artists of the important BRC since the 1980s. For a more sympathetic account of Presley's position and his effects, see Michael T. Bertrand, *Race, Rock, and Elvis* (University of Illinois Press, 2005).

8   Tim Riley writes, "When Elvis Presley leapt onto the popular stage … shaking his hips and singing with a new gusto and tenderness about love, he shattered prevailing notions about masculinity and femininity so completely that they never recovered." *Fever: How Rock 'n' Roll Transformed Gender in America* (Picador, 2005), xiii.

9   Veloso, *Tropical Truth*, 18.

10   Veloso, *Tropical Truth*, 23.

11   "They take the streetcar the day of tomorrow, they love their children the day of tomorrow."

12   Elijah Wald, *Dylan Goes Electric!: Newport, Seeger, Dylan, and the Night that Split the '60s* (Dey Street Books, New York, 2015).

13   For a more detailed account of this festival, its context, and its repercussions, see Christopher Dunn, *Brutality Garden*, 129–38.

14   Cited in Victoria Langland, "Il est Interdit d'Interdire: The Transnational Experience of 1968 in Brazil," *Estudios Interdisciplinarios de América Latina y el Caribe*, Vol. 17, No. 1 (2006): 61–81, 65.

15   Pedro Alexandre Sanches, "*Caminhando contra o vento, like a rolling stone*," http://revistacult.uol.com.br/home/2010/03/caminhando-contra-o-vento-like-a-rolling-stone/ (accessed 19 March 2017).

16   http://www.allmusic.com/album/a-foreign-sound-mw0000329917/ Deusner comes to a similar conclusion: "Veloso's version of Bob Dylan's 'It's Alright, Ma (I'm Only Bleeding)' —perhaps chosen for the relevance of its message—is a lamentable misstep." http://pitchfork.com/reviews/albums/8429-a-foreign-sound/ (accessed 19 March 2017).

17 See above, p. 45.

18 The drums on this track are by Pupillo, of the group Nação Zumbi, who mix Northeastern Brazilian traditional rhythms with rock, punk, funk, and hip hop in a sound known as *mangue beat*.

19 Though I highly recommend Billy Preston's, on *Everybody Likes Some Kind of Music* (1973)—very different!

20 Now, to be even more of a stickler, I correct not only the Nonesuch website, but my own note 1 in the Introduction: not only is this not Caetano's first album sung "entirely in English"—it's not actually entirely in English itself.

21 "É de perguntar se o espetáculo de anteontem, em que Caetano declarou sua identificação com a América—todo o continente, incluindo os EUA—não pode orientar essa leitura. Como na inserção, ao final de 'It's Alright, Ma (I'm Only Bleeding),' de Bob Dylan, dos versos—da canção de 'Deus e o Diabo na Terra do Sol'—'Se entrega, Corisco! Eu não me entrego, não.' Mas não, porque já estavam lá, dos versos de 'Love for Sale,' de Cole Porter: 'Quem está preparado para pagar o preço / de uma viagem ao paraíso?'" Rafael Cariello, "Nos EUA, Caetano Veloso iguala Bin Laden e Rice," April 18, 2004 http://www1.folha.uol.com.br/folha/ilustrada/ult90u43395.shtml (accessed 19 March 2017).

22 Robert Christgau calls Gil a "pop adept like Stevie Wonder," in contrast to Caetano and Milton Nascimento, whom he hears as "aesthetes like … Joni Mitchell." http://www.robertchristgau.com/get_artist.php?name=Gilberto+Gil

23 In fact, that entire album, *Stevie Wonder's Journey through "The Secret Life of Plants"*, is challenging. It combines a quirky, heartfelt spirituality and a scientific curiosity that have much in common with some of Gil's own concept albums.

24 "She's so young, and she misses the time in which a lot of people had cigarette lighters."

25 Simon Reynolds, *Rip It Up and Start Again: Post-Punk 1978–84* (Faber and Faber, 2005).

26 The song is featured in the 1981 film by Edo Bertoglio, *Downtown 81*.

27 Arto Lindsay's discography is extensive, but a telling spread of his solo work is collected on the double compilation album, *The Encyclopedia of Arto* (Northern Spy Records, 2014), which includes the gorgeous samba-bossa-soul-inflected work he created in the late '90s and aughts, as well as more recent live, stripped-down noise-guitar-and-voice performances with traces of his rawer vocal sound.

28 Veloso, *Tropical Truth*, 328–9.

29 In recent years, he's been designing and organizing parades, mixing his interests in the plastic, the performative, and the sonic. This work is influenced by his experiences in Brazilian carnival practices, as well as the *tropicália*-era street performances of Hélio Oiticica.

30 Simon Reynolds, *Rip It Up and Start Again*.

31 A few years ago, Caetano was approached, through David Byrne, by the fantastically imaginative young composer/producer Jherek Bischoff to sing on his album, *Composed* (Byrne also appears on it). Bischoff had a melody without words, and Caetano asked me if I might supply some. I suggested an adaptation of Rudyard Kipling's strange and wonderful poem, "The Secret of the Machines," which seemed perfectly suited to Bischoff's weird orchestral mix of mechanical and lush, overgrown sounds. The story of that poem is oddly similar to Byrne's lyric on "(Nothing But) Flowers." But in it, it's the machines of development themselves that narrate their power to create new ecological formations: "It is easy! Give us dynamite and drills! / Watch the iron-shouldered rocks lie down and quake / As the thirsty desert-level floods and fills, / And the valley we have dammed becomes a lake." It wasn't only the suitability of the imagery to the sound of Bischoff's composition that made me think it was appropriate for this project. I also loved the idea of Caetano singing "The Secret of the Machines," since his lifelong friend and collaborator, Gilberto Gil, had, as I've said, famously recorded a cover of Stevie Wonder's "The Secret Life of Plants."

32 David Byrne, *How Music Works* (McSweeney's, 2012), 33.

33 Ibid. 10.

34 As Christopher Dunn notes, this would lead to a tide of U.S. artists engaging with the music of *tropicália*, reaching its apex at the century's end (*Brutality Garden*, p. 204). In fact, the fascination continues. Numerous contemporary U.S. artists, from Beck to Devendra Banhart and Zach Condon, cite *tropicália*, and specifically Caetano, as an influence.

35 David Byrne, *How Music Works*, 62.

36 Albert maintains that the similarities are coincidental, but settled when Gasté sued.

37 http://istoe.com.br/12256_comvocesmauricioalberto/ (accessed 19 March 2017): "Eu compunha e cantava em inglês, meus ídolos falavam inglês, eram a nossa influência, e eu falava bem a língua, meus avós eram ingleses. O engraçado é que até hoje tem gente que pensa que eu sou americano, apesar de desde o começo eu fazer questão de dizer que era brasileiro … Me orgulho das minhas raízes, cantar em inglês não me transformou em um estrangeiro."

38 *Who Is Mr. Waxman?*, Ch. 2.

39 Hugh Barker and Yuval Taylor, *Faking It: The Quest for Authenticity in Popular Music* (New York: W.W. Norton & Co., 2007).

40 David Fricke, "Krist Novoselic on Kurt's Writing Process and the 'In Utero' Aesthetic," *Rolling Stone*, October 3, 2013. http://www.rollingstone.com/music/news/krist-novoselic-on-kurts-writing-process-and-the-in-utero-aesthetic-20131003 (accessed 19 March 2017).

Afterword

Eu quero dar o fora,
E quero que você venha comigo.[1]
CAETANO VELOSO, "VOCÊ NÃO ENTENDE NADA"

Eleven years ago, I had a sabbatical, and I decided to move back to Bahia for the semester with my son, who was twelve. I'd loved living on Mermaid Hill years before, and so I asked my son's father, who was Bahian, to keep an eye out for me if a house there should become available. He found one, a rickety little place perched precariously over a blooming jasmine bush. I bought it for about the price of a used car and had it fixed up. I moved in with my son. We were very happy there. We'd sit on the staircase next to a big window and watch the ocean spread out before us as though it were a movie screen. The soundtrack was the crashing waves, mixed with the occasional shouts of soccer players practicing down on the beach. Once in a while in the evening a little spontaneous samba would break out.

I was writing my first novel.[2] The narrator was a woman who taught Portuguese as a second language in New York. I'd done that myself. One of her students was a Japanese businessman named Mr. Tanaka, who was being transferred by his company to São Paulo. My narrator would sometimes use music to teach her students certain grammatical constructions, like, for example, the subjunctive. Her relationship with

Mr. Tanaka was pretty formal, but they shared some enthusiasms. She says:

> He's very into the music I give him. I burned him a CD with this beautiful song by Caetano Veloso called "*Você não entende nada.*"[3] The song is narrated by a guy who's pissed off about the stagnation of his life. He comes home from his shitty job everyday, oh, you know, *alienated*. He watches his wife cutting onions to cook with their dinner. She sets the table. She brings him a Coca-Cola. She serves the food. And he says, "*Eu como eu como eu como eu como eu como … você.*" I eat I eat I eat I eat I eat … you.
>
> He really loves her. He hates his job. He feels like setting fire to the fucking apartment. He wants to trash everything and hit the road. But he says to his wife, "And I want you to come with me." *E quero que você venha comigo*.
>
> *Venha* is the present subjunctive. You use it in these situations where you're expressing a desire that may or may not be fulfilled. Technically, you'd say, "And I wish that you might come with me."

Eventually Mr. Tanaka moves to São Paulo and something sad happens. He ends up taking a bottle of pills and calls my narrator in New York. She manages to get somebody to send the cops, but while she's waiting for them to arrive, she tries to keep Mr. Tanaka talking on the phone. She's afraid he's going to die and she's running out of things to say:

> Finally I thought of something. I said, "*Tohru, vamos cantar*

aquela música do Caetano que você gosta." Let's sing that song by Caetano that you like so much.

I started singing softly. It was very quiet. I wasn't sure he was listening. I sang a little more. Nothing. I paused. Then finally, tentatively, he came in on the line about the Coca-Cola.

We ended up in heartfelt unison on the refrain, which we kept repeating over and over, "*E quero que você venha comigo."*

And I want you to come with me.

We must have sung that song forty times. I heard the police arriving. Mr. Tanaka told me he had to go.

He was okay in the end.

I didn't know Caetano, but we had some academic friends in common, and they told me he'd read some of my academic writing about Brazil. I was surprised, but they said, "Oh, he reads everything. And he's always curious when foreigners are writing things about Brazil." I was living right on the other side of the hill from him. I wondered if he might want to know that a song of his had sort of saved my character's life. Thinking I had nothing to lose, I climbed, on foot, the long drive up to the upscale side of the hill and left my manuscript, with a note, with the security guard. I think I said something to the effect of, "I don't know that a song of yours has ever saved my life, but they've meant a lot to me." Weirdly, he read my strange little book, and wrote me after, saying he'd found it touching. He also said he'd been interested in my reading of "Haiti" in that academic book. I've bothered him since with my writings—in fact, often, after that, when I imagined a "dear reader," his was the sober, dignified, slightly skewed eye I would wish to fall on my text—estranged, but curious. And of course my own fascination with his music never diminished. My only hope is that I've been, or might be, a correspondingly strange but attentive listener. Dear reader, there you have it. My skewed but loving listening to your foreign sound.

Notes

1 "I want to get out of here, and I want you to come with me."

2 Browning, *Who Is Mr. Waxman?*

3 It's on *Caetano e Chico – juntos e ao vivo*, a concert recorded in 1972 with Chico Buarque, shortly after Caetano's return from exile.

Works Cited

Anonymous, "Goings on About Town," *The New Yorker* http://
    www.newyorker.com/magazine/2007/09/03/dance-21
    (accessed 19 March 2017).

Baldwin, James. *The Price of the Ticket: Collected Nonfiction,
    1948–1985* (St. Martin's Press, New York, 1985).

Baraka, Amiri. *Blues People: Negro Music in White America* (William
    Morrow, New York, 1963).

Barker, Hugh and Taylor, Yuval. *Faking It: The Quest for Authenticity
    in Popular Music* (W. W. Norton & Co., New York, 2007).

Barthes, Roland. *Image—Music—Text*, tr. Stephen Heath (Hill and
    Wang, New York, 1978).

Béhague, Gerard. "Rap, Reggae, Rock, or Samba: The Local
    and the Global in Brazilian Popular Music (1985–95)," *Latin
    American Music Review*, 27 (1) (2006), 79–90.

Ben. "How You Sound" http://positiveanymore.blogspot.
    com/2006/04/how-you-sound.html (accessed 19 March
    2017).

Bernstein, Charles. *Attack of the Difficult Poems* (University of
    Chicago Press, Chicago, 2012).

Bertrand, Michael T. *Race, Rock, and Elvis* (University of Illinois
    Press, Champaign, IL, 2005).

Braga-Pinto, César. "Supermen and Chiquita Bacana's Daughters:
    Transgendered Voices in Brazilian Popular Music" in *Lusosex:
    Gender and Sexuality in the Portuguese Speaking World*, eds.
    Susan Canty Quinlan and Fernando Arenas (University of
    Minnesota Press, Minneapolis, MN, 2002).

Brooke, James. http://www.nytimes.com/1993/08/12/world/
rio-journal-in-live-and-let-live-land-gay-people-are-slain.html
(accessed 19 March 2017).

Browning, Barbara. *I'm Trying to Reach You* (Two Dollar Radio,
Columbus, OH, 2012).

Browning, Barbara. *Infectious Rhythm: Metaphors of Contagion
and the Spread of African Culture* (Routledge, New York, 1998).

Browning, Barbara. *Samba: Resistance in Motion* (Indiana
University Press, Bloomington, IN, 1995).

Browning, Barbara. *Who Is Mr. Waxman?* http://www.
whoismrwaxman.com/ (accessed 19 March 2017).

Buarque de Hollanda, Heloísa and Gonçalves, Marcos A. *Cultura e
participação nos anos 60.* (Brasiliense, São Paulo, 1986).

Burns, Lori. "Genre, Gender, and Convention Revisited: k.d.
lang's Cover of Cole Porter's 'So in Love.'" Repercussions 7–8,
1999–2000, 299–325.

Bush, John. AllMusic Review http://www.allmusic.com/album/a-
foreign-sound-mw0000329917 (accessed 19 March 2017).

Byrne, David. *How Music Works* (McSweeney's, San Francisco,
2012).

Cariello, Rafael. "Nos EUA, Caetano Veloso iguala Bin Laden e
Rice," April 18, 2004 http://www1.folha.uol.com.br/folha/
ilustrada/ult90u43395.shtml (accessed 19 March 2017).

Castro, Ruy. *Bossa Nova: The Story of the Brazilian Music
That Seduced the World*, tr. Lysa Salsbury (A Cappella Books,
Atlanta, GA, 2000).

Christgau, Robert. "Caetano Veloso, *A Foreign Sound*" http://www.
villagevoice.com/music/we-got-a-lot-6407613 (accessed 19
March 2017).

Christgau, Robert. "Gilberto Gil" http://www.robertchristgau.com/
get_artist.php?name=Gilberto+Gil (accessed 19 March 2017).

Clarke, Donald. *Billie Holiday: Wishing on the Moon* (Da Capo Press, New York, 2002).

Crook, Larry. *Focus: Music of Northeastern* Brazil (Routledge, New York, 2009, 224).

Davis, Angela. *Blues Legacies and Black Feminism: Gertrude "Ma" Rainey, Bessie Smith, and Billie Holiday* (Vintage, New York, 1999).

Decker, Todd. *Who Should Sing "Ol' Man River"?: The Lives of an American Song* (Oxford University Press, New York, 2014).

Deusner, Stephen M. "Caetano Veloso, *A Foreign Sound*" http://pitchfork.com/reviews/albums/8429-a-foreign-sound/ (accessed 19 March 2017).

Dibbell, Julian. "Notes on Carmen," *The Village Voice*, 29 October 1991.

Dunn, Christopher. *Brutality Garden: Tropicália and the Emergence of a Brazilian Counterculture* (University of North Carolina Press, Durham, NC, 2001).

Dylan, Bob. *Chronicles* (Simon and Schuster, New York, 2004).

Farmer, Paul. *The Uses of Haiti* (Common Courage Press, Monroe, ME, 1994).

Freyre, Gilberto. *The Masters and the Slaves: A Study in the Development of Brazilian Civilization*, tr. Samuel Putnam (Random House, New York, 1964).

Fricke, David. "Krist Novoselic on Kurt's Writing Process and the 'In Utero' Aesthetic," *Rolling Stone*, October 3, 2013 http://www.rollingstone.com/music/news/krist-novoselic-on-kurts-writing-process-and-the-in-utero-aesthetic-20131003 (accessed 19 March 2017).

Friedwald, Will. *Sinatra! The Song is You: A Singer's Art* (Da Capo Press, New York, 1997).

Garofalo, Reebee. "Off the Charts: Outrage and Exclusion in the Eruption of Rock and Roll," in Rachel Rubin and Jeffrey

Paul Melnick, eds., *American Popular Music: New Approaches to the Twentieth Century* (University of Massachusetts Press, Amherst, MA, 2001).

Gershwin, George. "Gershwin explains why his *Porgy and Bess* is called 'folk opera.'" *New York Times*, November 2, 1935.

Gioia, Ted. *Love Songs: The Hidden History* (Oxford University Press, New York, 2015).

Gottlieb, Jack. *Funny, It Doesn't Sound Jewish: How Yiddish Songs and Synagogue Melodies Influenced Tin Pan Alley, Broadway, and Hollywood* (SUNY Press, Albany, NY, 2004).

Hanson, Alan. "Did Sinatra Really Bad Mouth Elvis and His Music in '57?" www.elvis-history-blog.com (accessed 19 March 2017).

Holder, Geoffrey. "That Fad from Trinidad," *New York Times*, April 21, 1957, 14.

Jones, Stacy Holman. *Torch Singing: Performing Resistance and Desire from Billie Holiday to Edith Piaf* (AltaMira Press, Lanham, MD, 2007).

Knight, Arthur. *Disintegrating the Musical: Black Performance and American Musical Film* (Duke University Press, Durham, DC, 2002).

Langland, Victoria. "Il est Interdit d'Interdire: The Transnational Experience of 1968 in Brazil," *Estudios Interdisciplinarios de América Latina y el Caribe*, 17 (1) (2006): 61–81.

Lehman, David. *A Fine Romance: Jewish Songwriters, American Songs* (Schocken, New York, 2009).

Leu, Lorraine. *Brazilian Popular Music: Caetano Veloso and the Regeneration of Tradition* (Ashgate, Aldershot, 2006).

Lévi-Strauss, Claude. *Tristes Tropiques*, trans. John and Doreen Weightman (Washington Square Press, New York, 1977).

Lott, Eric. *Love and Theft: Blackface Minstrelsy and the American Working Class* (Oxford University Press, New York, 1993).

McGowan, Chris and Pessanha, Ricardo, eds. *The Brazilian Sound: Samba, Bossa Nova, and the Popular Music of Brazil* (Temple University Press, Philadelphia, 2008).

Mahon, Maureen. *Right to Rock: The Black Rock Coalition and the Cultural Politics of Race* (Duke University Press, Durham, NC, 2004).

Melnick, Jeffrey. *A Right to Sing the Blues: Jews, African Americans, and American Popular Song* (Harvard University Press, Cambridge, MA, 1999).

Mercer, Kobena. "Reading Racial Fetishism: The Photographs of Robert Mapplethorpe" in *Welcome to the Jungle: New Positions in Black Cultural Studies* (Routledge, New York, 1994), 171–220.

Miranda, Ricardo. *"Autor de Feelings, música que o tornou famoso no Exterior, Morris Albert é o brasileiro que mais vendeu discos no mundo: 160 milhões de cópias,"* Isto É, July 7, 2004 http://istoe.com.br/12256_comvocesmauricioalberto/ (accessed 19 March 2017).

Moon, Tom. "Returning to Brazil in samba, hip-hop," *Philadelphia Inquirer*, April 29, 2001 http://articles.philly.com/2001-04-29/entertainment/25331641_1_noites-tropicalia-movement-bossa (accessed 19 March 2017).

Most, Andrea. *Making Americans: Jews and the Broadway Musical* (Harvard University Press, Cambridge, MA, 2004).

Murphy, John P. *Music in Brazil: Experiencing Music, Expressing Culture* (Oxford University Press, New York, 2006).

Nabuco, Joaquim. *Minha Formação* http://www.biblio.com.br/defaultz.asp?link=http://www.biblio.com.br/conteudo/Joaquim Nabuco/minhaforma%E7%E3o.htm (accessed 19 March 2017).

Nelson, Alondra. "Introduction: Future Texts," *Social Text*, 20 (2) (2002): 1–15.

Noonan, Ellen. *The Strange Career of Porgy and Bess: Race, Culture, and America's Most Famous Opera* (University of North Carolina Press, Chapel Hill, NC, 2012).

Obama, Barack. *Dreams from My Father: A Story of Race and Inheritance* (Times Books, 1995).

Pareles, Jon. "At Lunch with Caetano Veloso," *New York Times*, September 9, 1992 http://www.nytimes.com/1992/09/09/garden/lunch-with-caetano-veloso-lots-rebellion-little-hot-sauce-for-spirited-bob-dylan.html?pagewanted=all (accessed 19 March 2017).

PBS. "Broadway Musicals: A Jewish Legacy" http://www.pbs.org/wnet/gperf/broadway-musicals-a-jewish-legacy-about-the-film/1476/ (accessed 19 March 2017).

Perrone, Charles. *Masters of Contemporary Brazilian Song: MPB 1965–1985* (University of Texas Press, Austin, TX, 1993).

Perrone, Charles and Dunn, Christopher, eds. *Brazilian Popular Music & Globalization* (Routledge, New York, 2001).

Pop, Iggy, Veloso, Caetano, and Elling, Kurt. "Memorable Sinatra Moments," *New York Times*, December 11, 2015 https://www.nytimes.com/2015/12/12/arts/music/memorable-sinatra-moments.html?_r=0 (accessed 19 March 2017).

Ratliff, Ben. "JAZZ FESTIVAL REVIEW; Wily Mixer Of Cool Jazz, Brazilian Pop And High Art," New York Times, June 29, 1999 http://www.nytimes.com/1999/06/29/arts/jazz-festival-review-wily-mixer-of-cool-jazz-brazilian-pop-and-high-art.html (accessed 19 March 2017).

Reynolds, Simon. *Rip It Up and Start Again: Post-Punk 1978–84* (Faber and Faber, London, 2005).

Riley, Tim. *Fever: How Rock 'n' Roll Transformed Gender in America* (Picador, New York, 2005).

Risério, Antonio. *A Utopia brasileira e os movimentos negros* (Editora 34, São Paulo, 2007).

Rodgers, Richard. *Musical Stages: An Autobiography* (Da Capo Press, New York, 2009).

Rogin, Michael. *Blackface, White Noise: Jewish Immigrants in the Hollywood Melting Pot* (University of California Press, Oakland, CA, 1996).

Sanches, Pedro Alexandre. *"Caminhando contra o vento, like a rolling stone"* http://revistacult.uol.com.br/home/2010/03/caminhando-contra-o-vento-like-a-rolling-stone/ (accessed 19 March 2017).

Schwartz, Charles. *Cole Porter: A Biography* (DaCapo Press, New York, 1979).

Sears, Benjamin, ed., *Irving Berlin Reader* (Oxford University Press, New York, 2012).

Sinatra, Frank. *Playboy* Interview http://sinatrafamily.com/forum/showthread.php/29275-Frank-Sinatra-s-1963-Playboy-Magazine-Interview (accessed 19 March 2017).

Tatit, Luiz. *O Cancionista: composição de canções no Brasil* (Edusp, São Paulo, 1996).

Thevet, André. *Les singularités de la France Antarctique* https://archive.org/details/singularitezdela00thevrich (accessed 19 March 2017).

Vaz de Caminho, Pero, "Carta" http://www.culturabrasil.org/zip/carta.pdf (accessed 19 March 2017).

Veloso, Caetano. "Caricature and Conqueror, Pride and Shame," *New York Times*, October 20, 1991, H34.

Veloso, Caetano. *Noites do Norte* notes: http://www.nonesuch.com/albums/noites-do-norte (accessed 19 March 2017).

Veloso, Caetano. *O mundo não é chato* (Companhia das Letras, São Paulo, 2005).

Veloso, Caetano. "An Orpheus, Rising From Caricature," *New York Times*, August 20, 2000.

Veloso, Caetano. *Sobre as letras* (Companhia das Letras, New York, 2003).

Veloso, Caetano. *Tropical Truth: A Story of Music and Revolution in Brazil*, tr. Isabel de Sena (Da Capo Press, New York).

Vianna, Hermano. *The Mystery of Samba: Popular Music and National Identity in Brazil*, tr. John Charles Chasteen (University of North Carolina Press, Chapel Hill, NC, 1999).

Vinciguerra, Thomas. "The Elusive Girl from Ipanema: The endlessly covered Brazilian song turns 50 this year. What explains its quirky endurance?" *Wall Street Journal* (online), July 2, 2012.

Vogel, Shane. "*Jamaica* on Broadway: The Popular Caribbean and Mock Transnational Performance," *Theatre Journal* 62 (2010): 1–21.

Wald, Elijah. *Dylan Goes Electric!: Newport, Seeger, Dylan, and the Night that Split the '60s* (Dey Street Books, New York, 2015).

Whorf, Michael. *American Popular Song Composers: Oral Histories, 1920s–1950s* (McFarland, Jefferson, NC, 2012).

Wilk, Max. *The Making of* The Sound of Music (Routledge, New York, 2007).

Wilson, John S. "João Gilberto, Singer, Thrives in Understatement; Brazilian Guitarist Performs Bossa Nova Numbers at the Rainbow Grill," *New York Times*, October 15, 1968, 42.

Zinsser, William. *Easy to Remember: The Great American Songwriters and Their Songs* (Godine, Boston, 2006).

Index